D0558581

275

METAPHOR AND REALITY

Metaphor
& Reality

PHILIP WHEELWRIGHT

Indiana University Press

BLOOMINGTON & LONDON

FIFTH PRINTING 1973

FIRST MIDLAND BOOK EDITION 1968

Copyright © 1962 by Indiana University Press
LIBRARY OF CONGRESS CATALOG CARD NUMBER: 62-8971
Manufactured in the United States of America
ISBN 0-253-20122-5

TO

JEANE

on her twenty-first birthday

Preface

THE PRESENT book has grown out of a series of lectures given two years ago as Visiting Professor at the University of Bristol on the Churchill Birthday Foundation. For the opportunity of giving the lectures and for permission to publish them in this amplified form I offer acknowledging thanks to the University of Bristol, to Chancellor Sir Winston Churchill (whose far-sighted interest in humanistic studies made possible the setting up of the Foundation), to Vice-Chancellor Sir Philip Morris, and to Chairman of the English Department Professor L. C. Knights. Indeed, I am grateful somewhat beyond the reach of words to Professor and

Mrs. Knights for that remembered blend of intellectual light and hospitable warmth which furnished both stimulant and ambience for the lectures.

Portions of the material were later rearranged for lectures at the University of Frankfurt and the Free University of Berlin; acknowledgment is offered to the heads of the respective Departments of English, Professor Helmut Viebrock and Professor Heinz Reinhold. The students of English literature who participated in my seminar on *Four Quartets* at the Free University of Berlin are, alas, memories without names; but I wish they might know that our two-hour discussion of poetic images and meanings, with considerable attention to problems of translation, was peculiarly enlightening for me and therein contributive to the moulding of the book. How much might be gained if there were more of such interlinguistic attempts at "new criticism"!

At the University of Munich, in the *geistig-gemütlich* neighborhood of which I settled down to the job of converting lectures into chapters, Professor Wolfgang Clemen and Professor Helmut Kuhn, respective heads of the Departments of English and Philosophy, were most amiably helpful.

A grant from the American Council of Learned Societies facilitated the visiting of various libraries in Europe and the United States for purposes of research and validation.

Finally, let there be a special word of thanks to Professor Virginia L. Close, reference librarian of Baker Library, Dartmouth College, for her quietly intelligent help in various ways whenever needed. The appropriateness of this acknowledgment has been developing almost unnoticed over many years, and I am glad to declare it at long last.

P. W.

University of California, Riverside
January, 1962

Acknowledgments

ACKNOWLEDGMENT is made to the following publishers for permission to quote from the books indicated: Doubleday & Company, *The Poems of Richard Aldington;* Faber & Faber, Ltd., Edwin Muir *Collected Poems,* and the Aztec lyric in Irene Richardson *Fireflies in the Night / A Study of Ancient Mexican Poetry and Symbolism;* Harcourt, Brace, & World, Inc., T. S. Eliot *The Complete Poems and Plays 1909-1950,* Robert Penn Warren *Selected Poems, 1923-43,* and Richard Wilbur *Things of This World;* Alfred A. Knopf, Inc., *The Collected Poems of Wallace Stevens;* Liveright Publishing Corporation, *The Collected Works of*

Hart Crane; The Macmillan Company, *The Collected Poems of W. B. Yeats,* and John Masefield *Poems;* New Directions, *The Complete Collected Poems of William Carlos Williams,* and *The Collected Poems of Dylan Thomas;* Oxford University Press, translations of the two Vedic hymns in H. D. Griswold *The Religion of the Rigveda;* Small, Maynard, & Company, a lyric by T. E. Hulme published as an appendage to *Canzoni and Ripostes of Ezra Pound;* Viking Press, Josephine Mayer and Tom Prideaux *Never to Die/the Egyptians in their Own Words.*

Contents

METAPHOR AND REALITY

Introduction

THE SOLE excuse which a man can have for writing," says Rémy de Gourmont, "is to unveil for others the sort of world which mirrors itself in his individual glass." No doubt if we cared to quibble we could point to other and lesser excuses for writing, such as are assumed by makers of directories, committee reports, and literary excitants or sedatives. What the eminent critic had in mind, however, was the kind of writing which, whatever its particular incentives and aims, reveals the accents of a man speaking to fellow men. To speak forth honestly is to report the world as it is beheld (however precariously) in one's own perspective. Things have contexts, but only a person has perspectives. The essential excuse for writing, then, is to unveil as best one can some perspective that has not already become ordered into a public map.

The present book is concerned with the kind of writing that is radically perspectival. All writing, to be sure, is perspectival in the most general sense; for even the most banal cliché or the most plainly factual report is formulated from a certain standpoint, and represents a certain trend of associations and expectations. The difference is not between the perspectival and the universal; for every universal, at least every humanly intelligible universal, is perspectivally conceived. No, the difference is between perspectives that have become standardized and perspectives that are freshly born and individual. The latter are perspectives in the making, rather than perspectives already publicly established; it is with them that the following pages are concerned.

Let us be as clear as possible about the distinction, and about where the lines are to be drawn. In all important cases the lines will be blurred, for as the old Greek adage says, "You cannot cut fire with a knife." If for convenience we speak of open vs. closed perspectives, or (shifting from ground to medium) of fluid language vs. block language, there is no wish to pretend that we have a pair of clear-cut concepts. The distinction is best understood if block language ("stenolanguage") and fluid language are viewed as differing not so much in kind as in degree. The former may be conceived roughly as a limit toward which language tends as its connotative fullness and tensive aliveness diminish. Man, the user of language, is alive, and according as he lives more intensely his thoughts and utterances require language that can express their living form. Not that the language is ever quite adequate to the changing contours of thought; its triumph is brief at best. Moreover, even the most vibrant language must have its base of operations, which consists of repeated and repeatable thought-forms together with the linguistic conventions that normally express and indicate them.

But what is it to live intensely? The adverb is chronically misleading, for it is prone to connote, for many a reader, little more than neurotic excitement. There are various kinds of neural excitement, both good and bad, which is to say both imprisoning the mind in its psychic compulsions and sensitizing the mind for new awarenesses. The psychological concept by itself tells us nothing. Spiritual intensity is far more than neurotic excitement, and involves an independent dimension of experience; even though its material conditions and its overt manifestations may sometimes be hard for an outside observer to distinguish from other forms of behavioral abnormality. But outward and observational criteria are largely worthless where spiritual intensity is concerned. Yet it is not enough to speak of the testimony of the heart and let it go at that. For it is in spiritual matters that the Forgotten Enemy has set his most cunning traps. Self-delusion tempts us at every turn. How, if not by public observational methods, can we guard against the delusions of sheer subjectivity?

The two questions thus raised are intimately connected. The question, "What is genuine spiritual intensity?" and the question, "How to be independent of the world's stereotypes and yet to avoid the delusions of subjectivity?" represent different ways of framing the central human question. For intensity that is spiritual, rather than compulsive or sentimental, is not self-delusive; to wallow in self-delusion, while it may be pitifully human, is not spiritual. Let us employ the word "spiritual" in such a way that it does not on the one hand mean just another set of neuroses, and does not on the other hand precommit us to any theological or eschatological over-beliefs. Whether both one's neural constitution and an exudation of divine grace may perhaps have some ultimate relevance to the problem is not here in question. We are not dealing with ultimates; we are concerned with humanly graspable evidence. What in terms of human evidence is the meaning of spiritual intensity?

The argument that follows, while it does not employ the phrase "spiritual intensity," is really a sort of progressive implementation of the idea. The human problem at its highest pitch is the problem of living most intensely on the human level. The last phrase is decisive; sheer intensity for its own sake is no guarantee of value. Thus a sexual orgasm may be a very intense experience, but it does not in itself guarantee spiritual, which is to say fully human intensity. A spiritual intensity, while it does not deny or fear the rhythms of the body, is not subservient to them. Ideally there can be a harmony between the Dionysian dance and the Apollonian vision; but while Nietzsche tried to define such a harmony, his bumptious insights in *The Birth of Tragedy* succeed in doing little more than to call attention to the problem. For the problem cannot be defined, it can only be explored; and this, if anything, is the meaning of spiritual exploration. The intensity that is sought is an intensity of the focussed and uninhibitedly exploring mind; the next chapters, particularly Chapter III, will examine the semantic characteristics of such tensive and exploratory action.

Now action on the human level is symbolic action. Man is, perhaps uniquely, the symbolizing animal; he not only performs, he also means and intends and seeks to know. Somehow in the long temporal mystery of evolution there emerged the power and disposition to let something—whether a body, an image, a sound, or later a written word—stand as surrogate for something else. Therein man became—and neither anthropologist nor philosopher can say when or how—a linguistic animal.

To be a linguistic animal and to be a contemplative animal are two inseparable aspects of the human situation. One cannot contemplate, which is to say think about What Is, without employing language in some manner or other; and conversely the use of language, as distinguished from grunts and squeals, involves semantic pointers, which say something about, or at least raise questions about, What Is. Semantics and ontology are inseparable; the first is superficial without the second, which in turn is unintelligible without the first.

Several interpenetrating phases of the forthcoming argument may chiefly stand out: first, the role of language in all inquiry and in all attempts to grasp the nature of What Is; next the distinction between stereotyped language (block language, steno-language) and language that is alive, fluid, and (in the sense to be defined) metamorphic; next the emergence of sustaining symbols, including archetypal symbols, out of general metaphoric speech; next man's tendency to concoct myths, and the relation of this tendency to his metaphoric and symbolic modes of language and of thought; and lastly the characteristics of reality that suggest themselves when traditional modes of conceptualizing are put aside and the full connotations of tensive, expressive language are taken at face value. The final phase of the argument thus represents an attempt to explore the possibility of what, as distinguished from a metaphysics, may be called a *metapoetics*, which is to say an ontology not so much of concepts as of poetic sensitivity.

ONE

Language and Conception

WITHIN RECENT decades the problem of language has moved more and more into the forefront of philosophical inquiry. To be sure, the important of the problem had been partly recognized by various older philosophers, particularly whenever they had the wit and the intellectual modesty to perceive the ultimate impossibility of surrounding truth with firm bands of words. Thus Laotze, Confucius, Buddha, Socrates, Plato, and Aristotle in ancient times, Vico, Leibniz, Berkeley, and Schopenhauer in modern—to name but a few—would give intermittent attention to the linguistic problem in its relation to the wide-ranging inquiries that they wished to pursue. The noble warning with which the *Tao Teh Ching* opens—"The Tao that can be spoken is not the real Tao"—stands as probably the oldest clear expression of this basic semantic insight on record.[1] Nevertheless, despite such occasional recognitions of the semantic problem as an insistent intruder into philosophy, it is only within the last century, more or less, that the essential semantic substructure of conceptual thinking has been seriously and systematically explored.

There is a reason for this. The latter half of the nineteenth century was the time of a uniquely important set of discoveries. It was in this period that an eminent group of philological scholars, spurred and guided by the learning and energy of Friedrich Max Müller of Oxford University, succeeded in bringing to light, arranging, and putting into English translations the major literary and religious treasures of the ancient East. Half a century earlier Schopenhauer had discovered what he could of the *Upanishads* through a fragmentary and inaccurate eighteenth century Latin translation; after the labors of Müller and his colleagues it was possible for any interested reader of English without special linguistic equipment to read, in those fifty volumes constituting the *Sacred Books of the East,* as much as he might choose of the *Vedas,* the *Brahmanas,* the *Upanishads,* the *Bhagavad-Gita,* several of the *Puranas,* the *Zend-Avesta,* the *Diamond Sutra,* the *Tao Teh Ching,* and other classical records of ancient Eastern thought.

Granted that better and more readable translations of some of the works have appeared subsequently, still the great revolutionary impact upon Western thought—perhaps no less important in its social and cultural effects than the contemporaneous revolution that was going on in biology—was mainly the result of that initial set of exploratory translations.

For inevitably the semantic considerations of the seventeenth and eighteenth centuries had been primarily Latin-centered. Locke's analysis of "sub-stance," Kepler's comparison of *"anima"* and *"vis"* as alternative expressions for the force that is found in nature, and Schopenhauer's discussion of the meaning of abstract concepts all evince both the precision and the limited scope that are produced by a Latin-oriented way of envisaging semantic problems. Even when such imaginative thinkers as Vico, Hamann, and Herder sought to broaden the perspective by touching upon the relation of linguistics to mythology, they were limited by the fact that both terms of their comparison were almost entirely confined to Graeco-Latin materials. The newly explored myths and folktales of the American Indians, the Incas, and the South Sea Islanders had not yet found a suitably intelligible place in the still infant science of mytho-semantic inquiry.

But with the opening up, toward the end of the nineteenth century, of Oriental ways of thinking and expressing, the limitations of the Western liguistic perspective began to be more evident. Two factors, a negative and a positive, were principally influential.

The negative factor was furnished especially by the *Tao Teh Ching,* the *Analects,* and other writings of ancient China; for here were shown philosophical modes of inquiry, many of them of unmistakable depth and human relevance, which were carried on in a language—one could virtually say in two languages, a spoken and a written—radically different in construction and mode of functioning from the languages of the West. Grammatical parts of speech, which are so insistently flung at school children in the Western countries, can scarcely be said to exist here; noun-functioning, verb-functioning, and adjective-functioning are not clearly separate, and have to be judged from context. The positive factor, explored at great length by Müller himself, was found in the many analogies, hitherto unknown or imperfectly known, between Hindu and Iranian words and syntax on the one hand and those of the main Western languages on the other. Further details of such positive and negative evidences have been traced in a considerable number of books and need not be developed here.[2]

As a matter of fact, the real significance of the new linguistic discoveries revealed itself only slowly and controversially. The insights of Müller, often very penetrating, were discredited by scholars of the next generation who were antagonized by Müller's readiness to let certain favorite theories—the linguistic basis of myth in particular, and at one time the predominance of solar myths—run away with him. It has been mainly in the twentieth century that fresh semantic perspectives have received clear definition. The impetus and first indications provided by Oriental studies became supplemented by partially independent studies from at least three other directions: the anthropological, the neo-classical, and the philosophical. In anthropology the investigations of Lévy-Bruhl into the mental and linguistic peculiarities of so-called primitives, the examination by A. E. Crawley of the "holophrase" as characteristic of the speech and thought of American Indian tribes and other pre-civilized peoples, and the insistence of Malinowski, Lord Raglan and others on the relation between myth and ritual, and hence at least by implication to some extent between language and ritual, have been especially suggestive. In classical philology the investigations of Francis M. Cornford, begun with his early book *From Religion to Philosophy* and reflected in his translations of Plato, have furnished perhaps the main push toward a reconsideration of classical myth and classical doctrine in the light both of anthropological discoveries and of relevant modes of semantic analysis. In philosophy the most eminent work of a relevant sort has been done by Ernst Cassirer, who, beginning as a neo-Kantian and thus having undertaken to approach the problem of reality by the method of categorial analysis, has made in *The Philosophy of Symbolic Forms* a wide-ranging and often very penetrating study of the interrelations of sense-awareness, mental judgment, use of language, myth, and art.[3]

As a result there has been an increasing disposition in the twentieth century to bring the problem of language into the very center of philosophical studies. That is to say, language has come more and more to be regarded not only as a necessary means by which philosophical thought may be developed and communicated, but also as a basic ingredient of such thought. Consequently the traditional Cartesian dualism of mind vs. matter, or in its later forms subjective vs. objective, which has tended to give shape and direction to much of the philosophical thought since the seventeenth century, has begun to yield in many quarters to a threefold thought-structure, in which subject, object, and linguistic medium play irreducible and inter-causative roles in the formation of what, for want of a better name, we may call reality. The older epistemological dyad is becoming replaced, in much contemporary philosophy, by an epistemological triad. Letting S stand for the knowing subject, L for the language (in the broadest possible sense) by which S undertakes symbolic expression, and O for the meant or sought-for object, then the basic structure of any situation, so far as human beings can be aware of it or inquire about it, might be schematically represented thus:

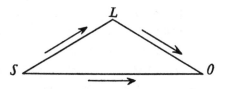

The point to be stressed is that neither S, L, nor O can be conceived as existing alone, apart from interplay with both of the other two factors. Often in a given situation, to be sure, emphasis and attention are given to one of the three factors in such a way that the implicit presence and influence of the others pass unnoticed. This may particularly appear to be the case when some object is investigated which we speak of as "an existing thing" and our attitude toward it is "purely objective." The height of a building, for instance, seems to be objectively what it is, independent both of subjective attitudes toward it and of the language in which it is spoken. And it is entirely true that *once this problem,* the height of a building, *has been clearly understood and formulated,* the determination of its height is purely experimental and objective in character from there on; neither subjectivity nor linguistic expression can then be admitted as having any essential relevance. However, the ability to inquire into the height of things and to know precisely what the problem means has resulted from a very long process in the evolution of human consciousness and of human measuring techniques. To have arrived at so definite a conception as a foot or an inch, and to have developed the technique of repeated superimposition by a standard length upon that which is to be measured, was an outstanding achievement of early human thought. If we can speak glibly of inches and feet nowadays, and can regard them as having an objective meaning quite apart from either mentality or language, our ability to do so is a result of a long process of early thinking in which both the subjective experience of height and length and the desire to communicate them by choosing standards of measurement played indispensable roles.

Even so objective a fact, then, as the length of a pencil or the height of a building owes its character in part to the shared spatial experiences of those who look and measure (S_1, S_2 . . .) and in part to the accepted conventions of measurement (L), whose role besides being practical is linguistic. "Nevertheless the length is what it is," the outraged realist may cry; "it is what it is, regardless of our varying optical sensations and accepted ways of marking lines on rulers!" Undoubtedly so, but the tautology gets us nowhere. Obviously what we want to know is not the empty truism that a building is as high as it is; what we want is an answer in terms of feet and inches, and such an answer always carries traces both of roughly shared subjectivity and of an exactly shared mathematical language. *A fortiori* when something less definite is the object in question—when, let us say, the thing under discussion is the character of a person, or the musical relationships in the Archduke Trio, or the ironically intermingled traces of evil, of accident, and of divinity in the world—then the interplay of O, S, and L is all the more evident and varied.

Granted then, as the foregoing illustrations show, that O involves both S and L, it is quite as evident on reflection that neither S nor L can stand alone. The subjective experience of awareness is outreaching, always expressing itself, however dimly, in some faith in and wonder about the world that extends beyond itself. And as for language, it can function as language only when there is a subject using it and a something to which it refers. All in all, then, the varying mutuality of the three factors may be asserted as an apriori postulate of any philosophical investigation.

Perhaps it will be objected that I am using the word "language" too broadly here, since it is taken to comprise not only verbal language, written and spoken, but also standards of measurement and (in part of what follows) images and gestures. However, what else can be done? Somehow the broadly linguistic factor in human experience must be conceived and named, and English vocabulary provides nothing better. In this broadest possible sense of the word "language" I mean to designate any element in human experience which is not merely contemplated for its own sake alone, but is employed to *mean*, to *intend*, to *stand proxy for*, something beyond itself. A standard of measurement has this characteristic, and is therefore in the broadest sense of the word linguistic. Gesture and ritual too, even though no words are spoken, may be linguistic; for except where they have degenerated into perfunctory and mechanical repetitions of bodily movements, they stand for, indicate, suggest, hence *mean* something more than themselves. Poetry is often linguistic on several levels at once; the precise sense in which a painting may be linguistic has been a matter of controversy in aesthetics; and it is a matter of controversy as to whether or not music may legitimately be considered linguistic at all. At any rate, the use of the words "language" and "linguistic" to indicate the broad sense in which something may be taken to stand for, represent, suggest, half reveal and half conceal something else, is justified by the fact that no other word in English can be used with the same intention without much greater dangers of misunderstanding and partisan interpretation.

The arrows in the preceding diagram indicate three aspects of what may be called the *semantic action* present in any human situation. The ambiguity of the word "mean," which can be used in sentences both of the form "I mean . . ." and of the form "it means . . .," finds some clarification here. The relation $S{\rightarrow}O$ signifies the most universal effort of the human mind when it is operating as a mind—the desire to know, to grasp, to have some kind of recognizable relation with What Is. But if a man is to intend What Is—that is to say, if he is to know it, or surmise it, or doubt it, or wonder about it—he can only do so through the instrumentality of language, as broadly defined. The linguistic instruments that he uses, which are part of his social heritage, at once make possible and set limits to the kinds of question he can ask, the kinds of reality he can conceive, and the ways in which he can conceive it. A person says, "I mean . . ." and what he wants to do thereby is define some aspect of O, and in the more important cases to establish his own place in the $S{\rightarrow}O$ relation. But his ontological intention is always partly frustrated by the fact that he is obliged to use language, and to conceive what he means in terms of language. However seriously he may want to reach out to know reality, he is always constrained to let some element of language do proxy for what he is trying to reach out to and know. He may then become aware that he is using language; and if he makes the language itself the object of his attention his question will then take the form of asking not what he himself means (i.e., is trying to grasp) but what the language means (i.e., stands proxy for). There is obviously a shift in the meaning of meaning as one passes from the syntax "I mean" to the syntax "it means." The implications of both forms of syntax must be retained. On the one hand the person himself wants to stand in relation to What Is, although he cannot avoid some dependence on language in so doing. On the other hand he must believe and feel that the language which he employs stands proxy for What Is; that the referential relation $L \rightarrow O$ is a real one, even though when he tries to *say* what L means he finds himself having to deal with a relation of the form $L_1 \rightarrow L_2$. Perhaps the answer is that there is inevitable frustration in trying to operate by speech alone. "What does friendship (L) really mean?" If this is a serious question and not merely a play for emotional satisfaction or a pedagogical request for translation into another language, a suitable reply will consist not of other words alone (L_2) but also in exemplifying friendship—i.e., giving it a place in living experience, which will have S, L, and O as mutually conditioning components.

TWO

Communication

THE TRIANGULAR diagram employed in the previous chapter is insufficient in one main respect. Although it represents the basic threefold relationship of knower, known, and linguistic medium, it ignores (merely as a first step in the inquiry) the indispensable problem of communication between one knower and another. Language is not exclusively a private concern; whatever the private subtleties and private values it may develop for a sensitive mind, there is always the inescapable question of how far one mind can share its insights and meanings with another. Referring to the diagram, we may now regard the left-hand apex, S, as becoming plural instead of remaining singular, with resultant ambiguities in O and resultant problems of effective expression in L. The problem takes somewhat different shapes according to the kind of communication that is sought—which is also to say, the kind of meanings that are to be communicated.

There is one broad class of meanings which offer very little difficulty of a philosophical kind; such difficulties as they occasionally engender being always removable—i.e., capable of solution—by a sufficiently good semantic method. Such meanings are those that I have elsewhere called *steno-meanings*[1]—which is to say, meanings that can be shared in exactly the same way by a very large number of persons—in general, by all persons using the same language or the same group of inter-translatable languages. Examples are so obvious that they may be mentioned without explanation. Common words like *child, parent, dog, tree, sky*, etc., are steno-symbols, and their accepted meanings are steno-meanings, because what each of the words indicates is a set of definable experiences (whether actual or only possible) which are, in certain recognizable respects, the same for all who use the word correctly. Moreover, the word has its sufficiently exact equivalent in Latin, French, German, Italian, etc.; we need not, at the moment, look beyond the language-systems of civilized Europe. Each of the common meanings can be made and kept exact by digital method—by pointing to examples.

Digital meanings are what St. Augustine is evidently discussing in the well-known passage in his *Confessions:*

> When my elders would name something and at the same time would move toward something, I would become aware of the connection and would perceive that the sound which they uttered stood for the thing they wished to indicate.[2]

Augustine goes on, to be sure, to mention the role which the bodily movements of his elders, as well as their facial expressions and tones of voice, played in establishing the meanings for him; doubtless these, when experienced or remembered by a sensitive child, would produce personal overtones that would go beyond the clear, everyday, and easily sharable meanings that could be understood by pointing. But it is not such connotative overtones that Augustine has here in mind, as is clear from his concluding sentence:

> Thus as I heard words used again and again in their proper places in various sentences, I gradually learned to understand what objects they signified; and after I had trained my mouth to form these signs I would employ them to express my own desires.

The triangular relation here consists of: $(S_1, S_2 \ldots)$ the inquiring child and the speaking, gesticulating elders; (L) the sounds as they are first heard and then reproduced by appropriate movements of tongue and larynx; (O) the familiar things in their common environment which can, for the most part, be pointed at.

Steno-meanings, or meanings that can be publicly and exactly shared, are not limited to objects and groups of objects in the immediate environment. They include sharable abstractions too. The method of acquiring these is, in general, an extension of the method that St. Augustine describes. Intermediate between concrete objects and abstract meanings there stand, as Plato has remarked,[3] the entities of geometry. They are abstract in that they have a perfection that is never achieved in actual experience, but they are concrete in that they can be conceived in visual terms. At the same time they are steno-meanings. A circle is a steno-meaning, because it is known in exactly the same way by all who understand geometry. Whether on a given occasion it is drawn with black pencil or white chalk is irrelevant; any imperfections in the drawing are irrelevant; the size and location of the particular circle are irrelevant. The essential property is that every point on the circumference must be equidistant from a given point which is its center; any actual circle is but an iconic sign for this meant and understood geometrically perfect circle—i.e., at once "imitating" it and indicating it. The essential circle, which is not visible in itself but which allows us to judge some visible figures as more nearly circular than others, is thus a steno-meaning of a semi-concrete sort—bearing toward actual circles an affinity that can be recognized by the visual imagination, and yet purified of the imperfections that inhere in what is actual.

But what is to be said of abstractions that are not geometrical and hence lack the demonstrable type of exactitude and objectivity of which spatial entities uniquely are susceptible[4]—e.g., justice, natural law, evil, divine providence, reality, etc.? Such terms are, in responsible discussion, made as precise as possible by definition and careful contextualization. When the discussion is carried on logically, an effort is made by all participants in the discussion, to use every such word in a single and understood sense. Although such words cannot have the kind of exactitude that belongs to a spatial entity such as the circle, the norm of shared exactitude is still employed in judging the logical merit of the discussion into which they enter. The acceptance and extension of that norm is indicated by Jesperson in one of his scholarly but conceptually limited treatments of language: "The ideal human language must be that which by the simplest and easiest possible means is able to express human thoughts in the fullest manner and in the manner easiest for the recipient."[5] Greatest ease for the greatest number! There, coming from an eminent philologist, is an avowal—perhaps more blunt and more extreme than many a steno-semanticist would care to accept—of the all too modern emphasis upon, and appeal to, what is publicly understandable and publicly explicable. To be sure, Jesperson adds the laudable condition that the thoughts are to be expressed "in the fullest manner," but the trouble is that fullness of expression and wide range of public intelligibility are contrary aims, which are generally found to be in conflict.

Social range is thus one of the motives of communication, and the cruder forms of its operation are evident in the bathos of modern journalism, conversational clichés, and popular art. In a more exact and carefully qualified way social range is also a motive in the building of scientific language. Thus the definition of a proton, for example, can be stated very exactly; and while there are questionable and disputed points about the behavior of protons, these too can be stated with exact estimates of probability. The number of persons equipped to understand the definition is limited, to be sure; but the point is that so far as they do understand it they can understand it in exactly the same way. That, at least, is the ideal of scientific definition. The experiences that two physicists have actually known in their experiments with protons are presumably different in various respects. Such differences, however, are irrelevant to the scientific question of how a proton behaves; from the standpoint of scientific semantics they are dismissed as "subjective"—i.e., outside the scientific problem as defined.

Briefly there are two ways in which steno-language, or closed language, language consisting of static terms, may arise: by habit and by prescription. Language becomes closed and static by habit when the imagination fails, so that the same words are repeated without examination or critical integrity. Such language has lost its vitality, as when a person talks too much about God or love or duty, or any other great theme. Language that is closed in this manner, by default, may be indefinitely susceptible of ambiguities; and such ambiguities, unlike the tensive ambiguities to be discussed in future chapters, serve no good purpose. When language is closed by stipulation, on the other hand, as is done in scientific and logical usage, the aim is to get rid of ambiguity as far as possible and to establish semantic precision combined with sharability by all "normal observers," or, in the case of technical matters, all "qualified observers." Language that is closed by stipulation—which is to say by definition, combined with a rigid adherence to the law of identity —may be called logical language. It is deliberate steno-language, as opposed to the accidental steno-language that enters into common speech.

When logical language is taken as the type of all valid language—that is, of all language in its representative role, as distinguished from language employed for the purpose of either emoting or persuading —the resultant philosophy (whatever other names may be given to it in certain of its particular developments) may be called *semantic positivism*. This philosophy involves as a corollary that the only legitimate role of any philosophy is to investigate and clarify the presuppositions, implications, and interrelations of the sciences; for it assumes that any inquiry into the nature of What Is can be valid—that is, can be composed of legitimate, meaningful questions—only so far as it goes about its task scientifically, which is to say, as a first step, only so far as it employs scientific, logical language. Thus one finds typically in the writings of semantic positivists the view expressed that logical language (consisting of both logical vocabulary and logical syntax) is the only language in which questions pertaining to truth can be asked, and that all other seeming questions are not really questions at all, but merely impulsive searchings for emotive satisfaction.

Now while logical language is manifestly of very great importance for situations and types of question to which it legitimately applies, its powers of reference are limited. To try to deal with all matters by logico-scientific language is as self-defeating as to try to capture water in a net, or a breeze in a bag. Meanings always flit mockingly beyond the reach of men with nets and measuring sticks. And the most vital problem of semantics (keeping the word in its broad sense, as the study of meanings) is, just how far and by what devices it is possible to give to such fluid uncaptured meanings some kind of linguistic expression.

Intelligibility is manifold. It can be simplified in an effort to be widely understood, and it can be confined with scientific responsibility to the kind of thing that publicly sharable experiments and observations are capable of indicating. In either case, however, something is left out. A definite whole is never *the* whole. Man's itch for truth cannot be entirely satisfied either by public agreement or by secure precision. There is also in man a desire, and it is a more enobling one, for greater fullness of knowledge, a yearning of the mind toward what lies beyond the reach of words as already used or as prescriptively defined. For this reason, however extensively and ingeniously any closed system or systems of language may be contrived, there will always be a need, so long as human imagination remains alive, to explore and develop the resources of open language.

But open language, the steno-semanticist (i.e., the semantic positivist) will retort, is necessarily vague, and therefore incapable of dealing adequately with questions of truth, which must be approached in his view by means of clear-cut concepts and exact logical relations. This is a fair statement, as brief statements go, of the position common to semantic positivists, by whatever name they may prefer to be called, and it must briefly be met before the main argument regarding open language can proceed. Let it be noted that there are two premises in the semantic positivist's argument: the major premise that exact language is the sole semantic means by which truth can be attained, and the minor premise that open language is necessarily inexact. The two assumptions invite separate examination.

First, is truth necessarily exact? In a technological age an affirmative answer is likely to seem self-evident to many persons, but such an answer merely expresses a collective prejudice of our time, a time in which the scientist has become priest. Neither logically nor historically is the affirmative answer self-evident. Logically it is obvious that the proposition, "Truth must be ultimately exact," cannot be proved; any apparent demonstration would commit the fallacy of question-begging, for it would have to be based upon an implicit definition of "truth" as having clear boundaries and hence as being ideally expressible in exact terms. But nothing is gained by going round in circles. Historically the case for the exactitude of truth is no firmer. It has not always, or even usually, been supposed that truth must be exact. "Nature loves to hide," says Heraclitus; Nietzsche expresses virtually the same idea in his suggestion that "Perhaps truth is a woman";[6] and Laotze begins his teaching with the declaration that "The reality (*tao*) that can be conceptualized is not the essential reality." Granted the practical as well as the occasional aesthetic values of precision up to a point and in ways relevant to a given problem, still it is possible that over-precision distracts a seeker from apprehending the object or situation in its full nature. Maximum exactitude, which is useful to the auto mechanic in understanding the relation of parts in a gear-shift or the flow of gasoline through the carburetor, is by no means possible or even desirable in a problem of personal relations; to insist too much upon exactitude in the appraisal of character or in the judgment of music would tend to blunt the sensibilities that are most necessary to such insights. But truths about human relations are surely as real and important (to say the least) as truths about gear-shifts and carburetors. It is needful to recognize, then, that there are kinds of truth to which the criterion of maximum exactitude is not applicable, and which can perhaps be referred to only vaguely, indirectly, and in soft focus.

Now what about the second premise in the semantic positivist's argument, that open language is necessarily inexact? The reply involves two complementary considerations. Negatively, it is true that open language cannot be as exact as responsibly closed language can be about the things and relations with which the latter properly deals. Nor can it be as exact *in the same way* as closed language is. On the affirmative side, however, let it be observed that a somewhat vague description or an indirect allusion may, with reference to a problematic situation, be more relevantly precise than the use of a more logical technique would be. To take a trivial example, suppose that someone's statement, "I prefer beef to mutton," is true—i.e., that it describes what is actually the case about the speaker's felt preferences. Suppose now that a captious critic were to demand greater exactitude, asking: *"How much* more do you like beef than mutton? Twice as much, or one and five-eighths as much, or just what?"* Such a question would probably be taken as a feeble jest; no sensible reply to it could be made, for the kind of exactitude it demands is apriori impossible in a situation that is not analyzable into identical units. Where more humanly important situations are involved—the sufferings of Oedipus, the ambivalent purposefulness of Hamlet, the tragic disorientation of mankind, the ambiguous conflict in a human relationship between love and egoism—the employment of alien forms of exactitude is *a fortiori* meaningless and absurd.

It does not follow, however, that open language must give up the quest for exactitude altogether. Language that is open may be loose and flabby, or it may be taut and alive; its openness is simply a general precondition. In order to speak as precisely as possible about the vague, shifting, problematic, and often paradoxical phenomena that are an essential part of the world, language must adapt itself somehow to these characteristics; the openness of the language permits such adaptation but does not guarantee it. Language that can adequately, or almost adequately, speak forth the living truths of human experience, must itself be living; and since those truths are always somewhat dark, kaleidoscopic and elusive, an appropriate language will to some extent, and with chosen controls, reflect those qualities. Wallace Stevens writes:

> The imperfect is our paradise.
> Note that, in this bitterness, delight,
> Since the imperfect is so hot in us,
> Lies in flawed words and stubborn sounds.[7]

But what of communication? All too often a poet's flawed words and stubborn sounds appear to some of his readers as a riddle without a key. Does not open language (so the common objection runs), even where highly satisfactory to its writer or speaker, fail to communicate its subjective meanings to others? Does it not tend, then, to become in effect little more

than an outlet for private feelings? Does not successful communication require, in the long run, language
that is scientifically exact?

But the problem of communication is not as simple
as that. All language, whatever its nature, has a communicative aspect; a part of its natural purpose as
language is to say something to someone other than
the speaker, even if the identity of that someone else
is not specifically known. Cases of talking to oneself
or of keeping a diary are derivative: they presuppose
a previous experience of communication with others.
But the possibilities are diverse. The communication
may be with one other individual, or with few or
many; it may be intended for human ears, or for the
souls of poets dead and gone, or for a daemon or god,
or for a transcendental Something-I-know-not-what.
In some communicative relations the language may
be of a secret and special kind, unintelligible to out-
siders. Ordinarily one is more successful at communicating fullness and intensity to a few persons of similar sensitivities than to a heterogeneous many. "Fit
readers find, though few," said John Milton, expressing every serious writer's hope. There is always risk,
for the fit readers may not actually be found, and at
best their fitness will be less than perfect. The risk is
the price that is paid for trying to speak with honest
and fresh imagination instead of dully falling into set
linguistic routines. How such fresh imagination affects
the characteristics of language, and how far such
imaginative language can deal with aspects of reality,
are questions that underlie the ensuing chapters.

THREE

Tensive Language

I⊤ IS NOT ENOUGH for language to be open; for open language may be loose, ambiguous, and ineffectual. The openness of language, so far as it exists, is valuable only potentially, only so far as it enables the language to be alive. Open language is not necessarily living language, but a certain restrained degree of openness makes linguistic life possible.

Now what is it for language to be alive? In all organic life there is a ceaseless but varying struggle between opposite forces, and without such struggle the organism would go dead. "Strife is the common condition," Heraclitus remarks, "and if strife were to vanish from amongst gods and men, then their very existence would cease."[1] In man the basic organic strife shows itself in various tensions, of which he may be unconscious or at most only partly conscious—the tension between self and other persons, between self and physical environment, between love and antagonism, between one's impulses and the decisions of rational thought, between the life-urge and the dark fascination of death. As man gropes to express his complex nature and his sense of the complex world, he seeks or creates representational and expressive forms (the two adjectives standing for complementary aspects of a single endeavor) which shall give some hint, always finally insufficient, of the turbulent moods within and the turbulent world of qualities and forces, promises and threats, outside him. His life oscillates between contrary pulls, and out of his Dionysian condition he seeks, and sometimes for lingering moments attains, an Apollonian vision. But if the vision is not to be escapist and a merely stubborn refusal to face things as they are, it will bear traces of the tensions and problematic character of the experience that gave it birth.

Thus language that strives toward adequacy—as opposed to signs and words of practical intent or of mere habit—is characteristically tensive to some degree and in some manner or other. This is true whether the language consists of gestures, drawings, musical compositions, or (what offers by far the largest possibilities of development) verbal language consisting of words, idioms, and syntax. A gesture in the worship of a tutelary daemon, or a phrase of the Lord's Prayer, is originally and properly alive and tensive. It may become commonplace and perfunctory through careless usage, which would mean that its original linguistic vitality had been lost so that its survival is merely a result of social habit; but when the gesture or the phrase reflects the religious aura that first surrounded it and gave it significance for an authentic worshiper, it has the power to elicit awe. Now awe is an ambivalent emotion, compounded of wonder and humility; the wonder keeps the emotion alive and the mind open, while the humility restrains the wonder from slipping into idle curiosity. In full human awareness there is likely to be a tension between these opposing and complementary tendencies, and any gesture or utterance that expresses such unspoiled awareness and craving for awareness will represent and convey something of that tension. When gestures, words, music or rhythms, and visible artifacts are combined in a pattern of liturgy, the same principle holds; except that now a larger amount of formalization and prescription comes in, and the degree of actual tensiveness will of course vary according to the sensitivity and disposition of the individual participant.

Where language in the more specific sense is in question—i.e., language as consisting of words and some kind of intelligible syntax—the problem becomes that of finding suitable word-combinations to represent some aspect or other of the pervasive living tension. This, when conscious, is the basis of poetry. Even in the simplest forms of poetic language some semantic tension can be discerned and felt, for without at least a flicker of tensive life the language would be semantically dead and therefore non-poetic, regardless of what the reputation of a work might be or what versifying ingenuity it might display.

> It's a strange courage
> You give me ancient star
>> WILLIAM CARLOS WILLIAMS

> Let us honour if we can
> The vertical man
>> W. H. AUDEN

> She walks in beauty, like the night
>> BYRON

> White in the moon the long road lies
>> A. E. HOUSMAN

> After great pain a formal feeling comes
>> EMILY DICKINSON

Imperfect illustrations all of them; for simplicity, if tensive, is never quite simple. There are subtle conflicts, and subtly different conflicts in each case. Poetic tension is of many kinds, and it need not be explicitly identified as tension by the reader who is enjoying the effects. Paradox, plurisignation, and wit-writing represent sophisticated developments of poetry, not its heartbeat. In order to discover the essential, and not be too easily distracted into sheer verbalistic analysis, we may remember the lesson of the triangle in Chapter I—a reminder that the verbal cannot be separated from the ontological and psychological factors in any real situation. If on the one hand Mallarmé was right in his declaration that "Poetry is not written with ideas, it is written with words," there is also the counter-warning of Lascelles Abercrombie aimed at those who speak too easily of "the magic of words—thereby pleasantly avoiding the necessity of thinking out what they really mean."[2] The two poets, coming at the problem from contrary angles, are alike in declaring that the music of the words and in some sense their meaning (which to Mallarmé would be a meaning created out of the magic of the words themselves) form a single problem—a tensively unified problem.

Recognizing, then, the essential and fluctuating togetherness of the three factors—of the poet who speaks, of the words in both their syntactical and their musical interrelations, and of the meaning that is suggested and aroused in the process—we can sometimes, without crippling the problem, shift the critical glance from one to another of them. Especially in trying to formulate the large sense in which poetry may be distinguished from the non-poetic, an ability to shift the focus of inquiry may prove helpful. For notwithstanding the truth of Mallarmé's proposition that poems are made with words rather than with ideas, it may still be that the essence of poetry is better defined in terms of *O* than of *L*. Poetic language is the first thing required if there is to be a poem, granted; but when the language of poetry is defined in terms of itself alone, there is little to say about it on the most general level except to mention the quasi-musical qualities which, in some manner or other, are expected to inhere in poetic language. This is not very satisfactory, and a poetry lover is likely to feel that the real point is being missed. For whatever are the analogies between poetry and music, and let it be acknowledged that they are important so far as they go, there is a difference too, which is no less essential. Music, for the most part, is self-contained; in the jargon of semantics, it is self-referring; it does not refer beyond itself to something that is meant, except in such vague ways as perhaps to suggest the quality of joyousness or of tragic seriousness in the world, or the hidden order beyond disorder, or the like. Words, by contrast, even in their most purely poetic usage, have a power of more specific eliciting; they not only *are*, they also *say*. And so it may be that a more suitable definition of poetry is to be found not by characterizing poetic language as such, but by indicating the general nature of that which is spoken of, when the speaking is truly poetic.

A phrase that would perhaps best indicate the most general characteristic of what is poetically disclosed would be *perspectival individuality*. Non-poetic language is not adapted to the unique; its natural reference is to ideas and perceptions that are publicly and easily shared. When a new slang phrase or a new descriptive epithet is born, it may sometimes have a slight poetic character for those who invent it or who first hear it, but it quickly falls into the rut of conventional speech, and when this occurs the poetic character vanishes. The conventional phrase conventionally employed is not remoulded and re-contextualized on each occasion of its use. Hence, even when there is novelty in the outlook of those who employ it, the phrase in itself does not contribute to the specific significance of that novelty. Poetic language, by contrast, does so contribute; it partly creates and partly discloses certain hitherto unknown, unguessed aspects of What Is. Every such aspect represents a perspective that is individual, that cannot be put into a class with other similar perspectives (except in abstract and largely irrelevant ways), and that is capable of eliciting a fresh response and fresh insight on the part of every attentive hearer or reader.

Even in the simplest cases of perspectival individuality there is semantic tension. A perspective is not an abstraction cut off by intellectual fiat from the conglomerate flow of experiences surrounding it; a good perspective, despite its light partisanship, will show qualities representing some aspect of larger reality. Its tensive character will be partly its own and partly drawn from the reality of which it is a part. Precisely here lies the difference between *mimesis* and logical abstraction. Consider the proposition: "There exist conflicting forces in nature, which interact according to physical laws." This is an example of abstraction. It is doubtless true enough as abstractions go; but what makes its truth possible? In order to be either true or false a statement must have meaning. Clearly, therefore, the quoted sentence relies for its possibility of truth upon the fact that readers or hearers of it will know, out of their own experience, what "conflicting forces" means. The sentence does nothing to create or enrich the idea of conflicting forces; it lives on borrowed semantic capital. That is, it states a probable connection between ideas that are already adequately understood. A ritual combat, on the other hand, is not abstract, it is mimetic. It, too, is partial; it represents only a certain aspect of experience; but it *represents by participating.* Those engaged in the ritual combat participate in the combative character of What Is, and thereby their dance has a representational and mimetic character. Hence the tension of the combat is caught up in the very gestures with which the combat is enacted. When words instead of gestures are employed, the mimesis of conflict can find a more indirect and more varied expression through rhythm and imagery and their attendant shifts of mood.

The twin aspects of tension and perspectival individuality operate at the simplest level in the achievement of that first and plainest of all poetic virtues— the expression of *radical actuality,* what Alan Watts has called the *suchness* of things, their precise character as actually observed. Radical suchness is hard to represent in words; the difficulty might be likened to that of a painter who with only a few colors on his palette should try to represent nature as he sees it. Painter and poet alike must resort to methods of indirection and suggestion. If a certain texture cannot be exactly reproduced on canvas, perhaps it can yet be forcefully suggested by stratagems of placing and contrast; sometimes, indeed, the impression of reality is even heightened by such limited formalizings. Gerard Manley Hopkins has given the name *inscape* to that immediate suchness as sensitively caught; he defines it as "the particularity of each unique thing as observed," and he illustrates his definition with the phrase, "Moonlight hanging or dropping on treetops like blue cobwebs."[3] The metaphor and the simile here are but instrumental; the intent and the main effect are directness. The perspectival individuality of the passage needs no comment; but wherein lies the tension? It consists, I would think, in the very contrast between the perspective, made suddenly real by the magic of the words, and the ordinary channels of thought and perception from which the mind has been summoned and to which it will return.

Words tend to slip away somewhat from the quality or scene they are intended to describe; the poet may then find means, analogous to the serious distortions of the painter, of introducing, as it were, counter-irritants.

> A boy with a dog before the sun, straddling
> Spontaneities that form their independent orbits,
> Their own perennials of light . . .[4]

Here, in "Sunday Morning Apples," Hart Crane makes an incisive grab at particularity. The tension subsists, to begin with, between that bright particular perspective and what lies outside the frame; further tensive interest is then given by the sudden introjection of abstractions; they are abstractions employed, however, not abstractly but mimetically—for their value in tossing oblique glances at the focussed scene. The sustention and development of a single quality upon which other qualities play (as distinguished from the interweaving of qualities, which is more often Crane's technique) is especially well illustrated in his "Garden Abstract," which achieves, in modern idiom, something reminiscent of what Marvell had achieved in "The Garden."

The tensive character of living language may be something more than the poet's choosing an individual perspective from which, at the moment, to look and to speak. There is always that much at least, when language is alive. There is always some tension, however delicate, between the bright center of particularity that is singled out for attention and the dim tail-of-the-eye impression of qualities and meanings and perspectives that was left out. That is why, when one reads a poem or a novel, even when it is of a straightforward kind, there is a certain quiet pleasure of exclusiveness, of being privileged to enjoy communion with a group of images or events or characters, which are simply and boldly just what they are and not something else. But in addition it is sometimes the case that tensive language owes its distinctive character to certain more special kinds of semantic action.

For one thing, there is always a certain vibrant relation between what is spoken and the living voice of the poet who speaks. Robert Frost has said that every poem is "dramatic" in the sense that someone is felt to be speaking it. Even though a good reader will give his main attention, and rightly so, to the poem itself as a presented composition, still the voice of the bard can be heard, however distantly, sparking the words. The voice is most prized when it is subdued, no doubt, and restrained from spilling into the poem the poet's raw emotions and opinions; nevertheless the voice, whatever its transmutations, still speaks.

Another kind of tension—one could say another dimension of it—arises from the overtones of universality that may be implied in an utterance. Such tension is typically found in the relationship, perhaps uncertain and wavering, between the situation as described or the succession of images as presented, and the stray glimpses of truth that they suggest without actually stating. It is in this sort of relationship that I. A. Richards' pair of words, *vehicle* and *tenor,* is most appropriately used: the one for the imagery or concrete situation described, the other for the ulterior significance that this suggests to the responsive imagination. But perhaps definition had better yield to presentation. Here are some utterances, diverse in source and intent, which have this one general trait

in common—that in each of them the imagery and
situation that are directly presented serve as vehicle
for a larger semantic tenor.

The lord whose oracle is at Delphi neither speaks nor
conceals, but gives signs.

HERACLITUS

You will not see the sky if you paint the glass blue.

ALAN W. WATTS

The promises of the Devil are kept to the letter and
broken in the spirit; God's promises are commonly broken
in the letter and fulfilled past all hope in the spirit.

COVENTRY PATMORE

> In a world of fugitives
> The person taking the opposite direction
> Will appear to be running away.
>
> T. S. ELIOT, *Family Reunion*

When we dream that we are dreaming, we are close to
waking up.

NOVALIS

> Let the snake grow wings.
>
> NAHUATL ADAGE

> Why put legs on a snake?
>
> ZEN ADAGE

Cast thy bread upon the waters: for thou shalt find it
after many days.

ECCLESIASTES

Water, the most humble of the elements, is content to flow downhill, offering no resistance; thereby it finds itself at last becoming one with the boundless sea.

LAOTZE

Poetic language generally, by reason of its openness, tends toward semantic plenitude rather than toward a cautious semantic economy. The power of speaking by indirection and by evoking larger, more universal meanings than the same utterance taken in its literal sense would warrant, is one species of semantic plenitude. But it may also be that the tenor of an image or of a surface statement is not single; the semantic arrow may point in more than one direction. When two such diversely intended meanings are sharply opposed, the result is paradox. But even when the doubleness of meaning is not pushed to the point of contrariety, it may often be the case that more than one meaning is suggested simultaneously by a certain word or phrase or image. Or, more characteristically, there may be a group of verbal symbols, put together in a certain syntax and suggesting certain images, some more overtly than others, with the result that the interplay of meanings and half-meanings is far more copious than any literal paraphrase could ever formulate. The greater instances of such plurisignation do not lend themselves to brief exposition, for they usually require patient analysis of an entire poem. On the other hand, a plurisign that is small enough to reside in a word or phrase is likely to seem, when shown out of context, to be little more than a pun or verbal trick. The example that follows, then, is of intermediate scope.

John Masefield's poem, "The Passing Strange," contains a small plurisign, to begin with, in its title. The phrase "passing strange" in traditional literary usage means "surpassing strange," which is to say "very strange indeed." But the opening stanza of the poem announces that another meaning is to be the dominant one:

> Out of the earth to rest or change
> Perpetual in perpetual change,
> The unknown passing through the strange.

Here the primary connotations of "passing" are *changing* and *impermanent*—an interpretation that is upheld as succeeding verses proceed to develop the theme of universal impermanence. But the ring of the word's other meaning, having been sounded in the title, will go on vibrating softly at the back of the reader's ear.

A subtler example of plurisignation in the poem can be observed in its references to the ancient but never dead symbol of wine. The symbol first appears in the third stanza. The second and third stanzas speak as follows:

> Water and saltness held together
> To tread the dust and stand the weather,
> To plow the field and stretch the tether,

> To pass the wine-cup and be witty,
> Water the sands and build the city,
> Slaughter the devils and have pity, . . .

Man is but water and salt, "mixed with the dust," and passing the wine-cup is but one of his many passing achievements, all of which vanish ultimately into the endless hollow of time. Yet wine, associated with the ancient idea of new life through mystical identification with the wine-god, carries also an overtone, however light and quiet, of that which somehow transcends and escapes the doom of universal change. This meaning, which is secondary in the third stanza, becomes dominant in the sixteenth:

> Since moons decay and suns decline,
> How else should end this life of mine?
> Water and saltness are not wine.

The main emphasis is now no longer upon wine as a part of the passing show, but upon the spiritual meaning of wine as distinct from the lesser substances, water and saltness.

The phenomenon of plurisignation has been recognized under various names by critics generally, but sometimes it has been defined inaccurately. Robert Bridges has gone to the length of declaring that all the particulars denoted by a word are brought into play in a poem. Similarly William Empson has said that all of a word's meanings and values are present when it is used poetically. Such statements push the matter too far. If they were true, then whatever meanings and values a word in a poem might have for any reader's rambling fancy would be a part of the poem's own meaning, and there could not be any question of whether the poem was being interpreted well or ill, suitably or arbitrarily. When in *The Waste Land* a reader confronts the lines—

> *Dayadhvam.* I have heard the key
> Turn in the door once and turn once only[6]

—he is struck, if he is poetically awake, by two overtones of meaning, one specific the other general in its power. There is the reference to Dante's somewhat melodramatic account of Count Ugolino's horrible doom in "the dread tower," and there is the vaguer but more inescapable reference to the ultimate loneliness of each human life. Both of these meanings are suggested by the language of the poem, not by the researches of lexicographers nor by the fancies of undisciplined readers. Yet the word "key" is polysemantic (what Bréal calls "polysemous"): it carries other meanings as well. It can be put to quite different uses in geography, in bookbinding, in masonry, and so on. Obviously Bridges and Empson, as practicing poets and intelligent critics, cannot have meant that all such uses of the word should be brought into play in reading Eliot's lines. But that, alas, is what they seem to say when their words are taken at face value. Far more accu-

rate, I should think, is Lascelles Abercrombie's statement that poetry, by its device of juxtaposition, de-
limits a "sector" of meanings, and thereby enriches
the word with "the individual vigor of some individual quality."[7] Interpretation is concerned not with
all the meanings a word might have, but with what
is revealed or hinted by the immediate passage and
the poetic context working in collaboration.

There are debatable cases, however. Another passage from *The Waste Land*—

> Who are those hooded hordes swarming
> Over endless plains, stumbling in cracked earth
> Ringed by the flat horizon only

—has a recognizable reference to the condition of
contemporary man, a reference which both the lines
themselves and the general purport of the poem con-
firm. To an American reader there is likely to arise
also some flitting memory of the white hooded Ku
Klux Klan. Is this out of place? Quite possibly the
poet had no such thought in mind; whether it affected subconsciously his choice of words cannot be
known. In any case the particular and regional horror
should not be allowed to make more than a tiny and
transient contribution to the general horror that is
intended. But I do not see how a southern negro
reader could altogether eliminate that local pictorial
reference from his awareness. Would he be misread-
ing the poetic line? Again, would a contemporary

reader be going astray if he were to think (lightly and unassertively, as all thinking about poetry should be done) of the scene as also potentially describing the remnants of mankind after a global holocaust? The thermonuclear aspects of such a notion could not have been thought of by the poet in 1925, but the general idea may have been. Besides, may it not be, and to what extent can it be, that the legitimate meaning of a poem grows and changes as the typical responses of fitly responsive readers change? But the question threatens to submerge us in circularity, for our initial query meant, in effect, just who *are* the fitly responsive readers? Specifically, what reader-responses to a given passage are most nearly adequate, as opposed to those that either force too much into the passage or draw too little out of it?

Controversy of an analogous kind has been stirred by the opening line of Part iii of "Burnt Norton":

> Garlic and sapphires in the mud
> Clot the bedded axle-tree.

The controversial word here is "garlic." Which image is intended—that of the white garlic flower, or the olfactory image of a rather pungent and sticky smell and flavor when garlic is put into foods? Some critics have rested their answer upon Eliot's report that the first line had been suggested to him by Mallarmé's *"Tonnerre et rubis aux moyeux"* ("Thunder and rubies in the mud"). But the meaning of a line is not limited to, and sometimes not even proximate to, what first stirred it in the poet's mind. Its significance in the composed poem is more to the point. John Malcolm Brinnin is nearer to the truth when he writes, "The sensory (*garlic*) and beautiful (*sapphires*) things of this world clot our vision of the still center which is God (symbolized by the axle-tree of the wheel which is also the axis of the earth)." Perhaps garlic has a general affinity with such uglier symbols in Eliot's poetic vocabulary as Mr. Eugenides the Smyrna merchant, Apeneck Sweeney erect, and the rat with slimy belly; while sapphires have a general affinity with the symbols of illusive and transitory loveliness, such as *la figlia che piange*, the hyacinth girl, and the rose garden. Grover Smith thinks that the garlic and sapphires "recall the mortal sins of gluttony and avarice"; perhaps they do, or might, but the idea needs to be muted and kept subsidiary, for if stressed it would blur out the paradox which the imagery of the first line contains. (If "garlic" were taken to mean only the white flower, instead of what is smelt and tasted, the paradox would be destroyed completely.) As for the second line there is also Elizabeth Drew's suggestion that "bedded" and "tree" may unite the ideas of manger and Cross. Grover Smith finds the suggestion an excellent one, on the ground that when the second line is so interpreted it "draws together the Atonement, the Incarnation, and the Passion."[8] Such a semantic outreach is appropriate enough to the movement of the poem, or to a large

aspect of it. Other critics, however, would reject the
interpretation as insufficiently justified by the imagery and context of the second line itself. The question is still, and will presumably remain, an open
one.

Uncertainty of interpretation might likewise settle
upon the word "toast" in Richard Wilbur's *Things of
This World*:

> But seeing rose carafes conceive the sun
> My thirst conceives a fierier universe.
> And then I toast the birds in the burning trees
> That chart their holy lucid drunkenness.[9]

If the word is taken in the context of *rose carafes,
thirst,* and *holy drunkenness,* it has one meaning; if
in the context of *fierier* and *burning,* it has another
and grimmer one. On the face of it, since the word
"toast" does in fact reside in the double context, it
might seem to be a focus of plurisignative meaning.
But since the breakfast-table associations of toast
seem inappropriate to the poem (a breakfast involving rose carafes and toasted birds can scarcely have
been intended!) should we then drop the idea of
plurisignation, and consider that the proximity of
"toast" to "burning" is mere accident? A poet of Mr.
Wilbur's excellence is not usually given to such careless mistakes. But the alternative is equally dubious,
and a reader cannot be sure.

The music of a poem may also contribute its share
to the expressive tensions that are engendered; which

is to say that various sorts of enlivening relations are possible between sound and sense. In general the sound of the words may act in either of two main ways: it may reinforce their intended meaning or it may pursue a pattern of its own, offering thereby a sort of quasi-musical counterpoint to what is meant. In onomatopoeia the sound of an utterance operates in the former way: in such words as "buzz" and "creak" it is tonal, and in such a word as "rickety" the reinforcement is rhythmic. Ezra Pound's "The Return" provides a remarkable example of sustained rhythmic reinforcement, while in Shakespeare's *Antony and Cleopatra* Enobarbus' description of Cleopatra's barge proceeding down the River Cydnus contains reinforcements that are both tonal and rhythmic.

> *Enobarbus:* I will tell you.
> The barge she sat in, like a burnish'd throne,
> Burn'd on the water. The poop was beaten gold;
> Purple the sails, and so perfumed that
> The winds were love-sick with them; the oars were
>   silver,
> Which to the tune of flutes kept stroke, and made
> The water which they beat to follow faster,
> As amorous of their strokes . . .[10]

The passage should of course be read aloud, with full value given to all the words. If the last three lines are read as the natural length of the syllables demands, the rhythm will be found to reinforce the meaning in "kept stroke" as well as in the quickening pace of the next line. The tonal reinforcements may be noted too. The strong *b*'s followed by the echoing *p*'s contribute both strength and lightness to the scene; while the liquidity of the ensuing vowels (provided the *u* of "tune" and "flutes" is allowed its full quality) has a special appropriateness both to the water in which the oars are splashily dipped and to the flowing sense of high passion that motivates both the river journey of the barge and the larger drama.

Such are some preliminary indications of the nature of tensive language. In developing and investigating further, since we cannot always be dealing with tensive language as a whole, it is desirable to look for a unit, or quasi-unit, of such language and one that shall be sufficiently representative. Three words have been put forward for the purpose in critical writings: *image, symbol,* and *metaphor.* Each of them has advantages, and each has certain drawbacks.

The word "image" has the advantage of emphasizing the most concrete element in a typical poetic situation. The suitability of its implied demand is seen in the fact that a poem without any imagery would not be a poem at all, but merely a versification of abstract ideas, like Parmenides' composition in hexameters, *On Truth.* C. Day Lewis declares that "the image is the constant of poetry, and every poem is itself an image." The reference, however, is evidently not so much to images in themselves, considered as sheer objects of contemplation, but rather to images with metaphoric potencies and metaphysical overtones. For in the very next sentence, after a word about the changing fashions in diction and attitude, Day Lewis concludes: "But metaphor remains, the life-principle of poetry, the poet's chief test and glory." Ezra Pound, too, prefers the word "image," and to him the image, in its poetic mode of functioning, is "an emotional and intellectual complex in an instant of time." And Allen Tate formulates the poet's problem when he asks how far an imagery can evoke a response that will issue forth "in a single act compounded of spiritual insight and physical perception."[11] Yet despite its effective use in critical discussion by such distinguished poet-critics as these, the word "image," when taken too universally, tends to prejudice one's attitude toward, and theory of, poetry. To some readers the word is likely to connote psychological subjectivity—elements in one's stream of consciousness instead of (what is to the point) their intended and suggested meanings and overtones. Moreover such usage may seem to lend critical priority to that special group of poets who have called themselves imagists and have elevated the importance of imagery beyond its due. Perhaps the most serious drawback of all is to be found in the critical difficulties created by an extension of the word "image" to cover the entire range of poetic expressiveness. Many a poem, such as *Four Quartets*, is built by alternately employing imagery and suppressing it; moreover it is important to be able to distinguish between the image and its tenor, inasmuch as either of them may be stable while the other varies. Discussion of poetry becomes artificially difficult if one's critical vocabulary sets up the word "image" as indicating the most basic category of poetry.

There are other writers, most eminently Goethe and Coleridge, who prefer the word "symbol." This word does, to be sure, have the advantage of insisting upon a semantic outreach, as the word "image" does not. As conceived by Mallarmé and his school, "symbol" meant at once the concrete image and its evocation of meanings and nuances that could not otherwise be articulated. So far, good. But often the implicit outreach of a symbol is regarded in too partisan a manner: Goethe, for instance, regarded a symbol as involving "the fullest coalescence of the particular instance and the general idea," which suggests a perhaps too great readiness to move in the direction of allegorical poetry; while according to Yeats the "great mind and great memory" of the world, the Anima Mundi, "can be evoked in symbols." Even if the special logico-mathematical use of the word can be ignored as too remote from poetic concerns to be misleading, it is still the case that for many persons the word "symbol" suggests meanings of a more permanent kind than those transient wisps of suggestiveness that are never entirely lacking in a poem and that sometimes mark its chief intent.

What, then, of the word "metaphor"? At first sight it might appear the least appropriate of the three words, inasmuch as most readers retain in their minds the

grammarian's definition of it. By its etymology, however, the word implies motion (*phora*) that is also
change (*meta*)—the reference being to semantic motion of course, not physical. As the next chapter will
show, the word can be employed and has been employed by certain serious critics in a wider and more
significant sense than the merely grammatical. "Metaphor is as ultimate as speech itself," writes John Middleton Murry, "and speech as ultimate as thought."[12] If
this is so, then *a fortiori* metaphor is essential to the living speech and thought that are poetry. In the elusive,
transitive state of critical vocabulary no solution can be
perfect; but at any rate the strategy of the next two
chapters will be, first to explore the fuller meaning of
the word "metaphor," and then to examine the conditions under which and the ways in which metaphor
thus broadly understood can develop into symbol.

FOUR

Two Ways of Metaphor

TAKING METAPHOR, then, as the element of tensive language that will serve best to reveal something of its nature, let us inquire with some care what metaphor is. The problem here, as in all serious definition, is to draw as usefully as possible the semantic lines marking off resemblances and differences. "Chop at the joints," both Plato and Chuang-tze have advised.[1] That is, let each definition correspond to some natural area of subject-matter, instead of being either arbitrary or a result of lazy convention. What, then, is the area of subject-matter for which the word "metaphor" can most usefully stand?

First, on the negative side, let it be noted that the grammarian's familiar distinction between metaphor and simile is to be largely ignored.[2] Strategies of grammar are not much to the point. Compare, for instance, Burns' line, "O my love is like a red, red rose," which is grammatically a simile, with the abbreviated statement, "Love is a red rose," which is grammatically a metaphor; probably it will be agreed that there is more tensive life, more metaphoric vitality, in the former than in the latter. Although it is often the case that a metaphoric comparison can be made more effective without explicit use of a word such as "like," it is not always so. The test of essential metaphor is not any rule of grammatical form, but rather the quality of semantic transformation that is brought about. Wallace Stevens, employing a somewhat different vocabulary, speaks of "the symbolic language of metamorphosis";[3] the purpose of such metamorphosis, he says, is to intensify one's sense of reality. It can scarcely be doubted that the simile of Burns' line does more to intensify one's sense of reality than the perfunctory metaphor that results from abbreviating it.

A more adequate and workable way of understanding metaphor must be sought, and of course it will not be anything as simple and rule-of-thumb as the grammarian's distinction. A clue is suggested by the idea, just mentioned, of metamorphosis. What really matters in a metaphor is the psychic depth at which the things of the world, whether actual or fancied, are transmuted by the cool heat of the imagination. The transmutative process that is involved may be described as *semantic motion*; the idea of which is implicit in the very word "metaphor," since the motion (*phora*) that the word connotes is a semantic motion—the double imaginative act of outreaching and combining that essentially marks the metaphoric process. The outreaching and the combining, which are the two main elements of metaphoric activity, appear most effectively in combination; perhaps, indeed, they are always combined to various degrees, at least implicitly. But as a means of understanding their respective contributions they may be examined singly, and may be called by distinguishing names —"epiphor" and "diaphor"—the one standing for the outreach and extension of meaning through comparison, the other for the creation of new meaning by juxtaposition and synthesis.

Epiphor

THE word "epiphor" is taken from Aristotle, who says in the *Poetics* that metaphor is the "transference" (*epiphora*) of a name [from that which it usually denotes] to some other object." [4] Although the bracketed words are supplied by the translator, it is clear enough from Aristotle's context that this is what he means. Epiphoric metaphor starts by assuming a usual meaning for a word; it then applies this word to something else on the basis of, and in order to indicate, a comparison with what is familiar. The semantic "movement" (*phora*) here is characteristically from a more concrete and readily graspable image "over on to" (*epi*) what is perhaps vaguer, more problematic, or more strange. "Life is a dream": here the idea of life, which is the tenor of the sentence, is relatively vague and problematic; whereas a dream is something of which, and of the waking up from which, everyone has memories. Accordingly dreaming can be offered as a semantic vehicle for those possibly similar aspects of life which it is desired to bring to the attention. Similarly, "God the Father," "the milk of human kindness," "his bark is worse than his bite," and so on; countless such examples of epiphoric metaphor, or epiphor, come readily to mind.

Since the essential mark of epiphor—which is to say, metaphor in the conventional Aristotelian sense—is to express a similarity between something relatively well known or concretely known (the semantic vehicle) and something which, although of greater worth or importance, is less known or more obscurely known (the semantic tenor), and since it must make its point by means of words, it follows that an epiphor presupposes a vehicular image or notion that can readily be understood when indicated by a suitable word or phrase. In short, there must be a literal base of operations to start from. When Edgar in *King Lear* says, "Ripeness is all," he is employing a word that has literal reference to a well-known condition of gardens and fruit; he is employing it as vehicle for a spiritual condition which is less easily described in literal terms, but which probably combines the ideas of maturity and of readiness (cf. the analogous remark in *Hamlet*, "Readiness is all"). Clearly this is a case of semantic transference. Since transference is perhaps the more conspicuous of the two elements in metaphor, it may appear to justify such a definition as that offered by Paul Henle: "A sign is metaphorical if it is used in reference to an object which it does not denote literally, but which has certain properties that its literal denotandum has." [5] This is Aristotle's definition couched in current academic terminology; the revealing thing about it is that there is taken for granted to be, at the outset of any metaphorical activity, a literal meaning, a standard usage, from which comparisons are drawn. And so there is—*to the extent that* the metaphor functions epiphorically.

But while it is true that an epiphor involves comparison as its central activity, and thus presupposes some kind of similarity between vehicle and tenor, it does not follow that the similarity need be obvious nor the comparison explicit. An already obvious resemblance would not provide any energy-tension; a steno-statement of comparison is not an epiphor. The best epiphors have freshness; they call light attention to similarities not readily noticed; they involve, in Aristotle's phrase, "an intuitive perception of the similarity of dissimilars." A tensive vibrancy can be achieved only where an adroit choice of dissimilars is made, so that the comparison comes as a shock which is yet a shock of recognition.

> A touch of cold in the autumn night
> I walked abroad
> And saw the round moon lean over a hedge,

Like a red-faced farmer.
I did not stop to talk, but nodded;
And round about were the wistful stars
With white faces like town children.

T. E. HULME, "AUTUMN"

All cries are thin and terse;
The field has droned the summer's final mass;
A cricket like a dwindling hearse
Crawls from the dry grass.

RICHARD WILBUR, "EXEUNT"

Behold my name stinks
More than the odor of carrion birds
On summer days when the heaven is hot.

Behold my name stinks
More than the odor of fishermen
And the shores of the pools where they have
fished.

EGYPTIAN, ANON., *circa* 1800 B.C.[6]

The possibilities of epiphoric development at the hands of an imaginative poet are numerous, and it would be futile to try to list them all. The purpose of criticism is not to set limits to the powers and discoveries of the creative mind, but to observe and not too assertively comment upon their results. A mode of epiphoric activity that is often intriguing is enclosed epiphor—the epiphor within an epiphor, and sometimes even another epiphor within that. Shakespeare offers a rich variety of such epiphoric enclosures, as for instance in Sonnet 65:

O how shall summer's honey breath hold out
Against the wrackful siege of battering days . . .

Youth is here described epiphorically as summer, and summer in turn as honey breath. The phrase "honey breath" may be analyzed in turn, for in it honey is a vehicle which epiphorically describes breath as its tenor. Here the semantic arrow points in turn from honey to breath, from breath to summer, and from summer to youth. Naturally such an analysis destroys the poetry of the line, for in poetry the relation of parts is organic, and it no longer looks the same when laid upon an operating table. But the threefold epiphoric relation is effectively present, even though its best work is being done below the horizon of consciousness.

Synaesthesis may sometimes add to epiphoric vitality, since the comparison of one type of sense-impression with that given by a different sense-organ stirs the reader to reflective contemplation along two of his avenues of sense at once. Some uses of synaesthesis, to be sure, seem to depend upon highly personal sets of associations, as when Rimbaud writes:

You vowels, A the black, E white, green U, blue O,
Some day I will reveal your hidden identities.

The comparisons here are so tenuous and personal that while the metaphor may be largely epiphoric to the poet, it can scarcely be other than diaphoric to most readers. There are other cases of synaesthesia, however, that appeal to more widely shared inter-sensuous associations in human experience. There is no difficulty in catching the meaning of such synaesthesiac epiphors as "a warm reception" and "a bitter reproach." Nor is a reader slow to perceive the difference between a person with "a blotting-paper voice," another whose voice is "like the beady eyes of a rattlesnake," and the heroine of whom a Mexican novelist writes, "Her voice was like the blue petals floating down from a jacaranda tree."

In general an epiphor is likely to have more life—which is to say more significance and more appropriate force—when it bears some recognizable relation to a large poetic area, whether to a local portion or to the whole of the poem in which it resides.

> The force that through the green fuse drives the flower
> Drives my green age; that blasts the roots of trees
> Is my destroyer.
> And I am dumb to tell the crooked rose
> My youth is bent by the same wintry fever.

In this passage from Dylan Thomas a single epiphoric theme is sustained through five lines, giving relevance and direction, therefore appropriate power, to the individual epiphors such as "green age" and "wintry fever." A distantly similar thematic usage may be found in some lines by the ancient Aztec poet Tochihuitzin:

> Like the grass renewed in the springtime,
> So we too acquire new forms.
> Our heart puts forth green shoots,
> From our body a few flowers grow,
> Then both become withered.

A more incisive logic of epiphoric development is found in Yeats' triple comparison:

> Shakespearean fish swam the sea, far away from land;
> Romantic fish swam in nets coming to the hand;
> What are all these fish that lie gasping on the strand?[7]

Diaphor

THE other and complementary kind of semantic movement that metaphor engages may be called diaphor. Here the "movement" (*phora*) is "through" (*dia*) certain particulars of experience (actual or imagined) in a fresh way, producing new meaning by juxtaposition alone. A trivial example may serve as a beginning. In a now forgotten little magazine of the thirties a leftist poet expressed his decidedly negative feelings toward America by publishing a poem which contained the following verse:

> My country 'tis of thee
> Sweet land of liberty
>   Higgledy-piggledy my black hen.

Leaving aside questions of worth and taste, let us note that in this combination of elements, and by their combination alone, the writer manages to convey what is not expressed by either of the parts. His intention is evidently to make an anti-patriotic utterance, but clearly there is nothing unpatriotic about either the first pair of lines taken by itself nor about the third line taken by itself. The anti-patriotic sentiment is expressed solely by their combination.

The purest diaphor is doubtless to be found in non-imitative music and in the most abstract painting; for wherever any imitative or mimetic factor is present, whether an imitation of nature or of previous art or a mimesis of some recognizable idea, there is an element of epiphor. The late Gertrude Stein was evidently striving as far as she could toward the purely diaphoric in such word-combinations as "Toasted Susie is my ice-cream," and "A silence a whole waste of a desert spoon, a whole waste of any little shaving. . . ." One could cite examples at random from Miss Stein's voluminous compositions. But of course such verbal diaphor cannot be as pure as diaphor in music can be. The words have off-stage meanings, and these impinge however fragmentarily upon the reader's mind. No one can deny, however, that Miss Stein has pumped them as empty of meaning as she possibly could; and it is instructive to note that in contriving such diaphoric word-patterns she considered that she was reducing poetry to the status of music. Indeed, the most effective use she ever made of her word-plays was in an actual musical setting; anyone who saw the memorable New York production of *Four Saints in Three Acts* in 1934 will remember "Which is a soon" and "Pigeons on the grass alas" not as abstract bits of nonsense, but as elements that entered into diaphoric combination with the richly lyrical contralto and tenor voices that respectively sang them, together with the freely haunting quality of Virgil Thompson's music,

with the dark skins and calm poise of the singers, and
with the pastel colored *papier maché* backgrounds.

It is almost impossible to find good examples of pure
diaphor that are not trivial, for diaphor does its best
work in combination, not alone. Presentation of contrast taken by itself becomes limited to immediate pictorial and musical interest; as soon as the contrast is
viewed in a larger context an element of epiphor peers
forth. Ezra Pound's "In a Station of the Metro" is primarily diaphoric:

> The apparition of these faces in the crowd;
> Petals on a wet, black bough.[8]

On first impact the pair of images seems to offer simply
an arresting contrast. The relation between them is presentational rather than representational. Any similarity
that a reader may find or think he finds between the
terms is not so much antecedent as (to borrow Henle's
pair of words) induced. Or, as William James would
put it, the association of ideas is based not on similarity
but on emotional congruity. All this surely is a plausible
way of taking the couplet.

And yet, while the imagery in the couplet is conspicu-
ously diaphoric, does it not perhaps carry an overtone
of epiphor as well? Visual awarenesses of the colors and
textures of the external world do vary, and possibly for
some readers there may seem to be a slight degree of
antecedent similarity in the contrast. It could be argued
that the juxtaposition is tinged, faintly and subtly, with

a suggested comparison. Moreover, both the diaphoric and the epiphoric elements are enlarged when the two-line poem is considered in the context of the other poems with which Pound has surrounded it. Petals have already been introduced in the three-line poem that immediately precedes, but the scene is altogether different; instead of the crowd in a modern metro there is the leisurely life of old China, marked by orange-colored rose-leaves and ochre clinging to stone in a fountain. Even in the more extended context the main impression is diaphoric; but there may also be a lightly breathed overtone of reference to the contrast between two human conditions, and to the extent that this is the case there would be a modicum of epiphor as well.

With the qualification admitted, and without insistence that diaphors must be entirely free from epiphoric admixture, there can be no doubt of the large and essential role that diaphor plays in poetry—the sheer presentation of diverse particulars in a newly designed arrangement. "Yes, to be sure," the conservative critic may retort, "the process is essential, I grant, but why call it metaphor? What is gained by extending the traditional meaning of metaphor to include mere presentational juxtaposition?" To this there are two replies. The first, my own, has already been indicated at the outset of the chapter; it rests on a need to see the two processes, epiphoric and diaphoric, as intimately related aspects of poetic language and as mutually contributing to the power and significance of all good metaphor. The other reply is indirect, by appealing to the independent insights of various students of poetry who, in whatever vocabulary, emphasize the diaphoric element in metaphor.

Northrop Frye, for instance, in his thoughtful study, *Anatomy of Criticism,* declares that metaphor "in its literal shape" is "simple juxtaposition"; and he remarks that "Ezra Pound, in explaining this aspect of metaphor, uses the illustrative figure of Chinese ideogram, which expresses a complex image by throwing a group of elements together without predication." He adds that predication belongs to "assertion and descriptive meaning," not to poetry functioning as poetry. Coleridge has coined the word "esemplastic" to designate the same kind of poetic activity, that of bringing diverse particulars into a newly established perspective; the poet being marked, he says, by a power to "diffuse a tone and spirit of unity that blends and (as it were) fuses each into each,"—a power that reveals itself in the balance or reconciliation of opposite or discordant qualities. Perhaps Shelley is not far off from this when he speaks of metaphoric language as marking "the before unapprehended relations of things." T. S. Eliot in a well-known passage is speaking not of the diaphor as it is revealed, but of the psychological process that precedes and enters into its making. As a comment upon "the apparent irrelevance and unrelatedness of things" that so often is found in poetry, Eliot remarks:

When a poet's mind is perfectly equipped for his work, it is consistently amalgamating disparate experiences; the ordinary man's experience is chaotic, irregular, fragmentary.

The latter falls in love, or reads Spinoza, and these two experiences have nothing to do with each other, or with the noise of the typewriter or the smell of cooking; in the mind of the poet these experiences are already forming new wholes.[9]

Side by side with such testimonies as the foregoing it will be useful to consider several of the definitions of metaphor offered by E. Jordan:

A metaphor is, then, . . . a formulation in words of the reality implicated in a variety that is conceived as a complex of qualities.

[A metaphor is] the assertion of an individuality; the assertion by which a complex of real quality becomes an individual or asserts itself as real.

[A metaphor is] a word-structure that, by virtue of its form, asserts the reality of an object. Form is here, as elsewhere, a system of mutually interrelating qualities which has effected a unity of its elements into a harmonious whole. This whole is the object which metaphor asserts.

The idea that metaphor expresses a likeness or a difference is perhaps a confused perception of the fact that metaphor always implies a variety of qualities in the reality it contemplates, but it appears to overlook the fact that the essential meaning of variety is not difference of quality so much as multiplicity of quality and the omnipresence of unlimited details of quality that are available for synthesis.[10]

In some instances a diaphoric synthesis is held together and as it were symbolized by a presiding image. Such an image may be chosen arbitrarily, by the poet's private sense of some hidden or potential congruence, or it may have some already recognizable relevance.

Wallace Stevens' early poem, "Thirteen Ways of Looking at a Blackbird," is an example of the former type;
its thirteen verses are related diaphorically, by pure
juxtaposition, and the presence of the blackbird in
each of them gives a sort of unity that is purely presentational, quite without any apparent epiphoric
significance.

i

Among twenty snowy mountains
The only moving thing
Was the eye of the blackbird.

ii

I was of three minds
Like a tree
In which there are three blackbirds.

iii

The blackbird whirled in the autumn winds.
It was a small part of the pantomime.

iv

A man and a woman
Are one.
A man and a woman and a blackbird
Are one.

v

I do not know which to prefer,
The beauty of inflections
Or the beauty of innuendoes,
The blackbird whistling
Or just after.

xiii

It was evening all afternoon.
It was snowing
And it was going to snow.
The blackbird sat
In the cedar limbs.[11]

When on the other hand the image that presides over
a diaphor has some recognizable significance—e.g.,
Eliot's presiding images of the Waste Land, the Rose
Garden, and the Still Point,—an element of epiphor is
thereby introduced. Each of the three images comes
into the poem already charged with partly understandable meanings and shared associations; in suggesting
them an image works epiphorically. As a poem *The
Waste Land* develops its effects largely by an often
abrupt synthesis of diverse images and situations: to
that extent it is diaphoric. But its presiding image (an-
nounced in its title) and many of the subordinate
images (e.g., Tiresias, the mock-Cleopatra sitting at her
dressing-table, the voice of the thunder, and so on)
work epiphorically as well.

The essential possibility of diaphor lies in the broad
ontological fact that new qualities and new meanings
can emerge, simply come into being, out of some
hitherto ungrouped combination of elements. If one
can imagine a state of the universe, perhaps a trillion
years ago, before hydrogen atoms and oxygen atoms
had ever come together, it may be presumed that up
to that time water did not exist. Somewhere in the
later vastitude of time, then, water first came into

being—when just those two necessary elements came together at last under the right conditions of temperature and pressure. Analogous novelties occur in the sphere of meanings as well. As in nature new qualities may be engendered by the coming together of elements in new ways, so too in poetry new suggestions of meaning can be engendered by the juxtaposition of previously unjoined words and images. Such diaphoric synthesis is indispensable as a factor in poetry. But the more interesting poetic moments are those in which it does not stand alone.

Epiphor and Diaphor Combined

USUALLY the most interesting and effective cases of metaphor are those in which there is in some manner or other a combination of epiphoric and diaphoric factors. The modes of combination are as various as the fertility of poetic imagination allows them to be, and the examples that follow indicate but a few of the many possibilities.

Auden's "The Fall of Rome" exemplifies a particularly clear division of labor between the two factors. Except in the last stanza the poem works mainly by epiphor: the theme of Rome's fall unmistakably speaks by indirection about the present state of civilization. But then at the end there is an abrupt leap, and the final verse without comment makes this simple contrasting statement:

> Altogether elsewhere, vast
> Herds of reindeer move across

> Miles and miles of golden moss,
> Silently and very fast.[12]

The diaphoric character of the sudden shift of scene becomes the more apparent when we try the experiment of inserting the word "But" at the opening of the first line. Observe how, by that small addition, the poetic impact is enfeebled. For whereas in Auden's version the quatrain enters diaphorically, making its point by sheer juxtaposition, the fancied revision sounds almost expository. The contrast becomes explicitly declared instead of being merely presented; as a result its diaphoric character is diminished and its epiphoric character is increased. For in that new version it seems to be declared a little too emphatically that those remote reindeer do stand for something—for some possible human condition vastly different from, and a relief from, that which is suggested by the fall of Rome. In Auden's version the epiphoric overtone, lighter and more subtle, is generated entirely by the diaphor itself, not by any particular verbal or imagistic vehicle.

A more frequent type of combination consists of a group of diverse epiphors serving as vehicles for a single tenor, the diaphor consisting in the fresh juxtapositions of the several vehicular images, as in this specimen of ancient reflective poetry from the Egyptian Pyramid texts:

> Death is in my eyes today:
> As in a sick man beginning to recover
> From a deep illness.

Death is in my eyes today:
Like the scent of myrrh,
Like sitting beneath the boat's sail on a breezy
   afternoon.

Death is in my eyes today:
Like a well-trodden road
Along which men are returning from foreign wars.

Death is in my eyes today:
Like the unveiling of heaven,
Wherein a man attains to that of which he had no
   conception.

Death is in my eyes today:
Like the desire of a man to see his home
After many a long year spent in captivity.[13]

An analogous method is sometimes employed in ancient philosophical writings, as when in the *Upanishads*
a diaphoric succession of epiphorically intended images
is offered as a means of inducing the mind to think
toward Brahma by a variety of inadequate approaches.
There is something to be learned, the Hindu *gurus* seem
to be saying, from recognizing the inevitable failure of
epiphor after epiphor to express the ultimate. Likewise
in such a passage as the following from the Chinese *Tao
Teh Ching* there is a diaphoric juxtaposition of particular epiphors, representing certain different angles of
vision converging upon the hidden, ever central reality
that is meant:

We put thirty spokes together and call it a wheel;
But it is on the space where there is nothing that the
   usefulness of the wheel depends.

We turn clay to make a vessel;
But it is on the space where there is nothing that the
    usefulness of the vessel depends.
We pierce doors and windows to make a house;
And it is on these spaces where there is nothing that
    the usefulness of the house depends.
Therefore just as we take advantage of what is, we
    should recognize the usefulness of what is not.[14]

Here the closing line may seem uncomfortably expository; to an agile mind the three images could have
spoken more forcibly by themselves, by their combined
suggestiveness, without pedagogic commentary. Probably that expository line operates in much the same way
as the proposed "but" in Auden's quatrain would have
done; both are intrusive, spoiling an otherwise balanced
interworking of epiphor and diaphor.

Sometimes the seeming epiphoric or diaphoric character of a passage may shift according to changing
poetic context. What looks in isolation like a diaphor
may prove to be epiphoric in relation to its poem as a
whole, and the reverse shift is possible also. The former
type of shift may be illustrated by considering the following bit of imagery:

> Are the halls of heaven broken up
> That you flake down on me
> Feathered strips of marble?

The juxtaposed images as they stand surely have a diaphoric look: they neither show nor ask any justification
beyond themselves. But see what happens to them
when they are set beneath the title that their maker

Richard Aldington had provided for them: "The Fawn Sees Snow for the First Time"![15]

The reverse relation may be illustrated by a pair of lines from Robert Penn Warren's "Pursuit":

> In Florida consider the flamingo
> Its color passion but its neck a question.[16]

The vivid irony of the two epiphors is the thing that strikes us immediately. "It's color passion" is a usual epiphor in unusual reversal. It is common enough to refer to passion by mentioning red or purple-pink, to serve as imagistic vehicle. Here a jolt is given by referring to the color, which now becomes the tenor, and letting passion (in whatever sense it may have meaning for whatever reader) stand as the vehicle. "Its neck a question" is jovially plurisignative. There is not only the obvious visual sense in which the flamingo's neck resembles a question mark; there is also the more contemplative sense, in which it is a question how so queer a neck can belong to a bird of such passionate color. On the other hand, all this snug epiphoric combination becomes diaphoric in the fuller context of the poem, wherein it enters abruptly in the fourth stanza, without comment, after imagery and scene of an altogether different kind—"the hunchback on the corner, with gum and shoelaces," followed by scenic jabs at a doctor's clinic.

Probably in the greatest cases of metaphor there is no clear division between epiphoric and diaphoric elements, but the two operate indissolubly as blended complementaries:

> My salad days,
> When I was green in judgment

> A bracelet of bright hair about the bone

> The wine of life is drawn, and the mere lees
> Is left this vault to brag of

> We have lingered in the chambers of the sea
> By sea-girls wreathed with seaweed red and brown

> Thou art a soul in bliss; but I am bound
> Upon a wheel of fire, that mine own tears
> Do scald like molten lead

Or ever the silver cord be loosed, or the golden bowl be broken, or the pitcher be broken at the fountain, or the wheel at the cistern—

That there is epiphor in each of the instances is shown by the felt subterranean power to mean something more than the words actually say. That there is diaphor is evident from the utterly untranslatable character of each utterance. The take-it-or-leave-it attitude that is implicit in all good metaphor is in itself, so far as it goes, diaphoric; the sense of an invisible finger ambiguously pointing is epiphoric. The role of epiphor is to hint significance, the role of diaphor is to create presence. Serious metaphor demands both.

FIVE

From Metaphor to Symbol

A SYMBOL, in general, is a relatively stable and
repeatable element of perceptual experi-
ence, standing for some larger meaning or set of meanings which cannot be given, or not fully given, in
perceptual experience itself. This broad definition is
intended to cover such diverse types of symbol as the
Bridge in Hart Crane's poem of that title, the mathematician's symbol π, the Christian Cross and the Buddhist
Lotus, Fire in the paintings of Orozco and in the philosophy of Heraclitus, and a historical culture-hero such
as Theseus or (with empirical impurities) Barbarossa

or (with yet more such) Abraham Lincoln. It is necessary to mention the stable and repeatable character of a symbol; for when an image is employed as metaphor only once, in a unique flash of insight, it cannot accurately be said to function symbolically. It acquires a symbolic nature when, with whatever modifications, it undergoes or is considered capable of undergoing recurrence. The Grecian urn in Keats' *Ode*, since it functions poetically by holding together certain imaginative experiences and possibilities of experience, which partly are expressed within the poem and partly are suggested as having a more universal life outside it, becomes the presiding symbol of the poem. On the other hand the "well wrought urn" in Donne's "The Canonization" functions on its one appearance in that poem as a metaphor rather than as a symbol; but when Cleanth Brooks employs the phrase as the title of a volume of critical essays he thereby transforms the metaphor into a symbol of another kind, functioning in an altered context. Similarly two metaphors from Donne's Sermons, "No man is an island" and "For whom the bell tolls," have become symbols in our time by reason of the wide currency that Ernest Hemingway has given them.

Now what is the difference between a tensive symbol such as Mallarmé's Faun, Crane's Bridge, and Yeats' Tower on the one hand, and the kind of symbol that is discussed in *The Journal of Symbolic Logic* on the other? The essential difference would appear to be twofold. First, the logician is free at the outset, at least in principle, to stipulate what a symbol shall mean for the duration of an investigation or argument; secondly, the logician demands of his symbols, at least in principle, that they shall have a public exactitude, an uncompromising identity of reference for all who use them correctly. Such symbols, which may be called "steno-symbols," are indispensable to science, and their frequent utility needs no demonstration. There are also steno-symbols of a more casual sort, where a metaphor has become rigid not through stipulation but through human inertia. Most of our common words or their synonyms in older languages have probably originated in this way, and in some of them the metaphoric origin can be seen or readily traced. Tensive symbolizing, on the other hand, is alive and does not proceed by stipulation even though human choice and discrimination contribute to it; nor is it ever perfectly exact—although it may, under favorable conditions, achieve a high precision. Let us look at these two characteristic differences of tensive symbols separately.

The tensive symbol cannot be entirely stipulative, inasmuch as its essential tension draws life from a multiplicity of associations, subtly and for the most part subconsciously interrelated, with which the symbol, or something like it and suggested by it, has been joined in the past, so that there is a stored up potential of semantic energy and significance which the symbol, when adroitly used, can tap. Absence of stipulation need not mean, however, absence of poetic choice. Crane exercised choice when he took Brooklyn Bridge as the presiding symbol for his major poem. Doubtless he could have found some other element in the American landscape that might have served much the same general purpose. But whatever presiding image he might have chosen for a poem about America, his choice would have affected the center of gravity of the poem, and a different presiding image would have required an appropriate alteration of lesser images, scenes, and developments. A mathematician is under no such responsibility. If some other Greek letter, not π, had originally been chosen to represent the ratio of circumference to diameter of a circle, the mathematical relations and laws would not have been altered a whit thereby; but if Shakespeare had decided to let the Weird Sisters inhabit water, like the Rhine Maidens, instead of "fog and filthy air," the whole play of *Macbeth* would have been profoundly different.

In the second place, the tensive symbol cannot be altogether exact. The meaning of π has to be exact absolutely and on all mathematical occasions. But the meaning of a tensive symbol allows to some degree both soft focus and contextual variability. Because of the nutritive darkness of proto-semantic experience in which it has taken root, and also because of its aim, which is to represent and evoke something of the richness and wonder and mystery of the world, a tensive symbol will allow some degree (preferably not too much) both of obscurity and of variation in the responses of awareness that it calls forth. Carlyle is speaking about tensive symbols when he writes that "in a symbol there is concealment and yet revelation, . . .

silence and speech acting together." Likewise Wallace Stevens when he declares, "The poem must resist the intelligence almost successfully."[1]

The distinguishing line between tensive symbol and steno-symbol is sometimes, to be sure, uncertain. What of the Cross, or the Flag? Each of them was once a tensive symbol, and it can still be such for the fit believer. But fit believers are few, and the average American churchgoer, seeing the two artifacts standing in uneasy conjunction in the chancel, accepts them as a matter of course, much as he accepts the minister's earnest adjurations and the familiar moan of the hymns. "It is the tendency of all symbols," the late Dean Inge has remarked, "to petrify or evaporate, and either process is fatal to them."[2] It would seem likely that both the Cross and the Flag have become, for most people most of the time, loose steno-symbols. Their originally tensive character, for first century Christians and responsible participants in the American Revolution respectively, has ordinarily either hardened into a bludgeon or, for people of a more tolerant sort, evaporated into air.

A poet's way with symbols is by recontextualizing to give them new life. In choosing a presiding image to function symbolically in a poem, shall the poet prefer a traditional symbol that requires renovation or a new symbol that has not been sullied and weakened by previous use? Dante's major symbols illustrate the one answer, Stevens' blackbird the other; Shakespeare's imagery involving tempests illustrates the one, his Caliban the other.

Dante stands supreme in his genius for transmuting Christian symbols and Christian dogmas into great poetry. The activity of Christian symbolism in the *Commedia* is too large a subject, however, for present discussion. More readily instructive, because less heavily organized, are the Christian symbols in Shakespeare's *Richard II* and *Macbeth*, in the later and occasionally the earlier Donne, in Blake, Hopkins, and Eliot. What all such authentic instances show, despite their diversities, is that Christian symbols, to be poetically effective, need to be discovered afresh in new contexts of imagery and of phrases. Christian blessedness is indicated in *Macbeth* chiefly by symbols of disorder, darkness, violence, and confusion, which connote its absence; these are set, moreover, among secular image-symbols and event-symbols ("the tempest-haunting martlet," the somnambulism, the natural dialectic of tyranny, etc.) which have their source in regions of experience outside of Christianity. Eliot's recontextualization of the Christian symbol of the Dove by momentarily identifying it with a bombing plane and the first of Yeats' "Two Songs from a Play" ("I saw a staring virgin stand/Where holy Dionysus died . . .") offer striking contemporary examples.

Outside the Christian framework the symbols principally available for sustained poetic use are those which have already received earlier literary expression, so that they come into the new poem equipped with a set of associations that will be largely intelligible to the literate reader. Historical events can be employed symbolically too, as in Marvell's "Horatian Ode" and

Yeats' "1919"; but here the poet has to assume that the events in question will be understood and evaluated by his various readers in much the same way that he intends. Past literature, on the other hand, including myths in proto-literary guise, offers the advantage of greater definiteness; it furnishes, to a degree, textual evidence of what certain symbols formerly meant and can again perhaps partially mean. Symbols having a literary background and a consequent potentiality of allusive reference may be described as having ancestral vitality.

By the definition on which the foregoing discussion has been based, symbol is distinguished from metaphor by its greater stability and permanence; but these qualities are more marked in some symbols than in others. Steno-symbols, as already remarked, have acquired either a passive stability by habituation or a rigid fixity by abstraction and stipulation; they lie, therefore, outside the present problem. The analogous question, for them, is the merely empirical one, of how widely the actual utility of a word or sign extends: thus *cat, Katze, chat,* and *gato* do service for those who speak the appropriate language, π for those who know mathematics, etc. But concerning tensive symbols it can also be asked, although more problematically, How wide-ranging is their power of suggestion and evocation? What is the social extent of their expressive function? Comparing tensive symbols in this way we can discover five main grades of comprehensiveness, or breadth of appeal. A symbol may complete its work as the presiding image of a particular poem; it may be repeated and developed by a certain poet as having special importance and significance for him personally; it may develop literary life ("ancestral vitality") by being passed from poet to poet, being mingled and stirred to new life in fresh poetic contexts; it may have significance for an entire cultural group or an entire body of religious believers; and finally it may be archetypal, in the sense of tending to have a fairly similar significance for all or a large portion of mankind, independently of borrowings and historical influences.

1. *The presiding image of a single poem.* Examples of this first type of tensive symbol are found where the symbol has not had any literary or cultural ancestry, and where it has not yet become influential outside the poem. As negative instances: although the symbol of Metamorphosis has been employed by Ovid and that of the Waste Land by Eliot, each as the presiding image-idea of its respective poem, yet each of the two meaning-complexes has had considerable life and usage outside as well. Metamorphosis is a potent philosophical and literary image-idea from Heraclitus to Joyce, and the Waste Land symbol (through no fault of the poet) has subsequently become glibly employed by moralists and amateur sociologists. Mallarmé's Faun and Hart Crane's Bridge are purer examples. Brooklyn Bridge— "implicitly thy freedom staying thee"—having airy affinity with the rippling rest, the dip and pivot of the soaring seagull, becomes for the reader of the poem a symbol of vast and somewhat focussed but untranslata-

ble power. Its meaning has to be drawn from many images, with their half-suggestions of idea; and these idea-
images are related with various degrees of affinity and
contrast, the latter amounting occasionally to paradox.
For on the one hand the Bridge in its freedom and
unspent motion is contrasted with the Wall Street gird-
ers and the derricks of iron city lots beneath it; yet
paradoxically the Bridge itself is one of the means by
which the once free bay waters playing around the
Statue of Liberty have become "chained." These and
other such explicit symbols of freedom and enchainment
appear in the Proem; the memory of the Bridge, with
what it implies concerning the hope and tragic degradation of the American dream, remains active as a semantic undercurrent through all the later scenes of the
poem, with their regional survey of the eastern half of
America.

In a shorter poem by Crane, "Praise for an Urn," the
presiding image would seem to have a double focus; it
comprises both the urn itself and, more essentially, the
memory of the dead friend whose ashes the urn holds.
The poem is a funeral ode, and with the restraint of
skilful indirection it is tight with grief. Appropriately it
contains intermingled suggestions of life and death.
Such phrases as "the slanting moon on the slanting hill"
and "the dry sound of bees / Stretching across a lucid
space" are evidently employed not merely in diaphoric
contrast to "the insistent clock of the crematory lobby,"
but presumably represent certain memories shared with
the dead friend. The synthesis of death and life elements is epitomized in the final stanza:

Scatter these well-meant idioms
Into the smoky spring that fills
The suburbs, where they will be lost.
They are no trophies of the sun.[3]

What are the well-meant idioms? Primarily, no doubt, the ashes in the urn, which are to be scattered. But "well-meant" and "suburbs" suggest a secondary meaning too. What of the well-meaning mourners who, when the funeral is over, will return to the smoky spring of their suburban houses, where presently life will ramble on again as if nothing much had happened? Thirdly, as an overtone at least, the well-meant idioms are doubtless the idioms of the poem itself. In all three senses the scattered idioms are set in contrast to the bright Apollonian orb which, throughout its long poetic life, has connoted both permanence and healing.

The last example shows how difficult it is to draw suitable boundaries around the scope of a symbol. The urn derives much of its symbolic power, of course, from associations that are independent of the poem. It is chosen as a presiding image for the reason that it is already a symbol of death. On the other hand, the urn in Crane's poem is not the same as the urn of either Donne or Keats. The character of the urn is subtly transmuted by its association with the loss of a friend and his reduction to ashes, and by the grief that permeates these ideas. The urn out of context, viewed as having a character in common with other urns, would be an abstraction. What matters is that this particular urn together with the felt death of a loved one, the degradation and the grief, all combine to make a total significance that eludes full speech. On the other hand, even when a symbol belongs somewhat uniquely to a particular poem, it does not, if it is truly effective, stay confined there. Moby Dick cannot remain confined within Melville's novel; as Northrop Frye has remarked, "he is absorbed into our imaginative experience of leviathans and dragons of the deep from the Old Testament onward." [4] Any tensive symbol is likely to have lurking potencies of indefinitely expanded reference.

2. *The personal symbol.* Hart Crane, who stands as perhaps America's finest lyricist, can also furnish an example of the second kind of symbol—that which has continuing vitality and relevance for a poet's imaginative and perhaps actual life, and which recurs in various forms from time to time in his poems. In the "Cutty Sark" section of *The Bridge* there occurs the following pair of lines:

> Murmurs of Leviathan he spoke
> And rum was Plato in our heads.

The outward scene into which the passage enters is a South Street bar where the poet is sitting with a green-eyed sailor, who drinks rum with him and talks of the "high intensity of the seas." A jukebox is playing "Stamboul Nights," a popular song of the twenties. The Stamboul Rose of the song becomes transformed into "Rose of Stamboul—O coral Queen" and then into "Atlantis Rose."

ATLANTIS ROSE drums wreathe the rose,
the star floats burning in the gulf of tears
and sleep another thousand—

The mention of Atlantis gives new significance to the
earlier phrase, "And rum was Plato in our heads." There
is of course a general and familiar sense in which rum,
if sipped as the accompaniment to enlivening conversa-
tion, can make the drinker become, or at least seem to
himself, more philosophical; that is no doubt a contributing part of the meaning. But there is no evidence in
Crane's poems or letters that he was interested in Plato
or Platonic philosophy in its larger aspects. What inter-
ests him here is Plato's particular teaching, in the
Timaeus, about the ancient kingdom of Atlantis, sunk
in its entirety under the sea. It had been—so Plato
affirms, following an ancient Egyptian tradition, and so
Crane also wants to believe—a kingdom in which justice, beauty, and intellectual life were actively furthered by good laws and sound principles of education.
But before the known era of history began there were
vast global changes and the ancient island-continent of
Atlantis sank beneath the sea; so that nowadays the
burning star must float in the waters of sorrow and
frustration, while "drums wreathe the rose." The craving for justice and beauty must "sleep another thousand" years, or however much longer; and Atlantis, the
archetypal realm of uncorrupted bliss, must lie dormant
among coral wreaths at the bottom of the ocean. Crane's
prepossession with the Atlantis symbol shows itself in

the underseas imagery that he develops in "At Melville's Tomb" and elsewhere, and perhaps it may bear some relation to his final act as a man, when in April 1932, a few minutes before noon, he leapt from the stern of the S. S. *Orizaba*, about three hundred miles north of Havana en route to New York. Whatever his other reasons may have been, it was symbolically a leap toward the locale of his dominant Image.

A poet's predilection for some dominant image need not, of course, find any such manifestation in his outward life. Knowing nothing of Shakespeare's outward life, we still cannot miss the power and intended meaning, in his plays and sonnets, of music, jewels, gardens, good earth, the noble horse, and ordered government, contrasted with tempests, confusion (and "confounding"), rude sounds, stinging adders, fawning dogs, and plotting rebels. Some of these symbols he brings in embodied form on to the stage, others not; all of them play their several roles in the developing imagery of the Shakespearean writings, from the Sonnets to *The Tempest*. And while some of them have had periods of symbolic life before and after Shakespeare, the uniquely woven pattern of associations arising from their combination is the master's own. The differentiation between personal and general symbols can be seen more plainly in Henry Vaughan's use of the symbols White and Light. The former is mainly personal, and its power and meaning are developed through accumulated instances—the purpose of the Incarnation, "to make stain'd man more white than snow"; the high dead as "white pilgrims"; the Patristic Age as "those white days"; and one's individual childhood as having been filled with "white celestial thoughts." Light, on the other hand, which is even more characteristic of Vaughan's imagery, is an archetypal symbol, of virtually universal human range.

3. *Symbols of ancestral vitality.* The phrase "ancestral vitality," as already proposed, may be applied to symbols that are lifted by one poet, for his own creative purposes, from earlier written sources. The special semantic enrichment that is made possible by such borrowings comes from the diaphoric merging of certain past meanings with such new meanings as are indicated by the context into which the symbol is freshly introduced. Eliot's *The Waste Land* contains perhaps as generous a number of instances as any modern poem. The slack, lush modern harlot with her mirrored dressing-table reflecting her jewels, with her strange synthetic perfumes and her neurotic inertia, draws much of her significance from the strongly suggested contrast with the queenly figure, moved by a more robust passion, of the Shakespearean Cleopatra. What mainly impels the contrast is Eliot's adroit parody of the description that Shakespeare has assigned to Enobarbus (here quoted in Chapter III) of the royal concubine as her barge is rowed, in leisurely grandeur, along the River Cydnus. In place of Shakespeare's strong *b* sounds, with their light echoes in the ensuing *p*'s, followed by liquid consonants and *u*'s that iconically evoke the water and the flutes, and then the quick *t*'s that

mark the stroke of the oars,—in place of the wonderful semantic entourage that Shakespeare has contrived for that ancient embodiment of royal lust, this modern courtesan is pegged on a more debased imagery—the original "barge she sat in" becoming the "chair she sat on," and "burned on the water" becoming "glowed on the marble, where the glass . . ." The deliberate slackening effect of the *ch-* and *gl-* sounds is made possible by the remembered contrast of that earlier, more valiant version.

Since Eliot is, of all modern poets, probably the one who has most conscientiously and persistently explored the allusive possibilities in poetry (if we omit Joyce's prose creations as belonging to another category), it is particularly worthwhile to observe his different kinds of allusive strategy. One notable difference may be observed between those allusive symbols that refer only to a given passage in a poem or play and those that refer at once to an earlier passage and also through it to stories or other sets of meanings involved in it. When the only reference is to the older literary passage itself, the process consists of an epiphoric reaching backward in order to produce a fresh quality from the peculiar diaphoric combination. The symbol of a Game of Chess, in *The Waste Land,* is an example. It stirs a backward look toward *The Tempest,* Act V, where redeemed Prince Ferdinand and Miranda express the intellectual harmony of their coming union by playing at chess, and secondarily toward the cynical seduction scene in Middleton's *Women Beware*

Women. Eliot's reference to playing a game of chess, while "pressing lidless eyes and waiting for a knock upon the door," draws its power of irony from the combined play of the two allusions. In the allusion to *The Tempest* the ironic contrast is direct, and of much the same analogical quality as the contrast between Elizabeth and Leicester beating oars in a gilded shell and the modern Thames sweating oil and tar, or that between the Rhinemaidens and the harlots of Margate; but in the allusion to Middleton the irony is oblique— a theatrical reminder that seduction was done in a more highly polished fashion then than now. The resultant quality that the Chess symbol has achieved is complex, but the complexity does not point beyond the two literary prototypes themselves.

Take, on the other hand, the mention, also in *The Waste Land,* of the nightingale and the cock. The representation of the nightingale's song as "jug jug" suggests an intended reminder of Lyly's *Campaspe:*

> What bird so sings, yet so does wail?
> O! 'tis the ravish'd nightingale.
> *Jug, jug, jug, tereu,* she cries,
> And still her woes at midnight rise.

But the Lyly passage is incidental, and a reader loses very little by not having known it; the important thing is that he shall know, especially in Ovid's breezily melodramatic version, the full story of King Tereus' rape of his sister-in-law Philomela and her eventual metamorphosis into a nightingale, together with the significance of the accusatory cry "tereu" and the inarticulate "jug jug" from the wounded tongueless mouth.

Again the description, in Part V of *The Waste Land,* of the cock on the deserted chapel roof, lighted up for an illusory moment by a flash of lightning, is doubtless meant to stand in ironic contrast with the cock in Kyd's *Cornelia:*

> The cheerful cock, the night's sad comforter,
> Waiting upon the rising of the sun.

But behind both Kyd's play and Eliot's poem there lies the long recognized symbolic plurisignation of the Cock. He has four characteristics that have set him off by their symbolic suggestiveness: his faithful crowing at the end of each night to usher in the dawn, his red comb which is an ancient icon of the sun supplemented by a later reference to Christ's redeeming blood, his noisy sexuality (hence, by free symbolic logic, his potency) which he expresses by crowing in triumph after coition with a hen, and finally the Gospel story of the cock's crow in relation to Peter's denial of Christ. Here are pagan and Christian elements jumbled together; it is not certain how far each of them should be stressed in a reading of *The Waste Land;* but they hover in the background, offering potential forces of association.[5]

4. *Symbols of cultural range.* The last example just given might as easily be put into this fourth class of symbols—those which have a significant life for members of a community, of a cult, or of a larger secular

or religious body. Eliot's use, in *Four Quartets*, of such transmuted Christian symbols as the wounded surgeon and the dying nurse, Adam as "the ruined millionnaire," the dripping blood and bloody flesh, the "prayer of the one Annunciation," the Dove, and the imposed choice of "either fire or fire," provides as rich a pattern of instances as can be found in modern literature.

Generally the richest field of shared symbolic materials, for members of a Christian or quasi-Christian society, is to be found in the Bible, particularly in the King James Authorized Version. To be sure, where the symbolic vehicle is a narrative episode, such as the temptation in the Garden or the building of the Tower of Babel, it makes little difference what translation is employed, and the Revised Standard Version has some manifest advantages of accuracy and intelligibility. But where the very idiom and accentual strokes of the utterance enter into the tone and suggestiveness of what is said, it is likely to be the older translation that has the more effective cultural range. "And they heard the voice of the Lord God walking in the garden in the cool of the day." The quiet sense of transcendent presence that has become associated with the utterance in this form is surely somewhat weakened by the revisionists' single alteration of "voice" to "sound." Again, "For dust thou art, and unto dust shalt thou return;" how much of the full tensive communication is lost by shifting from this to the matter-of-fact tone of the revisionists' "You are dust, and to dust you shall return"! What is in question here is not the degree of proximity to the original Hebrew text, but simply how the compared phrases tend to function for an English reader sensitive to nuances and having some acquaintance with the living traditions of English prose and verse.

In the New Testament it is the Fourth Gospel, the gospel according to John, which offers the greatest treasure of Christian symbolic material. Here Christ is represented by several prominent images: as the Door ("By me if any man enter in, he shall be saved, and shall go in and out, and find pasture"), as the Bread of Life ("He that cometh to me shall never hunger"), as the true Vine ("As the branch cannot bear fruit in itself, except it abide in the vine; no more can ye, except ye abide in me"), as the Word (the opening verses of the Gospel), and, most archetypally, as the Light. The metaphor of the Door has not been developed into a symbol in Christian liturgy or iconography, as has happened to each of the others in one way or another. The Bread and the Vine, on the other hand (the latter in the aspect of Wine) become central to the sacrament of Holy Communion; the Word and the Light have become familiar ingredients in Christian theology, prayer, and poetry. Each of the last four symbols had a precursory symbolic life before Christianity, but they receive new meaning in the Christian context.[6]

5. Finally there are *archetypal symbols,* or *archetypes*—that is, symbols that have an identical or similar meaning for mankind generally or at least for a large part of it. The nature and problems of the archetypal symbol require a longer discussion, and hence the subject is reserved for the following chapter.

SIX

The Archetypal Symbol

THE FIFTH CLASS of symbols, the archetypal, consists of those which carry the same or very similar meanings for a large portion, if not all, of mankind. It is a discoverable fact that certain symbols, such as the sky father and earth mother, light, blood, up-down, the axis of a wheel, and others, recur again and again in cultures so remote from one another in space and time that there is no likelihood of any historical influence and causal connection among them. Why should such unconnected repetitions occur? The reasons are in many cases not at all puzzling. Despite the great diversity among human societies and their ways of thinking and responding, there are certain natural similarities too, both in men's physical and in their basic psychical make-up. Physically all men are subject to the law of gravitation, for which reason *up* is normally a more difficult direction in which to go than *down;* and this makes it natural enough that the idea of going up should associate itself with the idea of achievement, and that various images connoting loftiness or ascent should associate themselves with the idea of excellence, and often of regality and command. Hence everyone finds it natural to speak of "striving upwards," and not of "striving downwards." A king rules "over" his subjects, not "under" them. We speak of "surmounting" our difficulties, and we triumph "over," not "under," temptation. Various images that are empirically associated with the idea of *up*, such as a flying bird, an arrow shot into the air, a star, a mountain, a stone pillar, a growing tree, a lofty tower, come to mean (whatever the other meanings that may have got attached to one or another of them) something to be reached for, a hope of attainment, hence in some sense the Good. *Down,* in one of its two main types of context, connotes the opposite idea. We "fall" into bad habits or into bankruptcy, we do not climb into them. In religious symbolism the image of the Abyss, with its attached sense of abrupt downwardness, is reinforced by man's deep-lying dread (as can be demonstrated empirically with infants) of falling, of sudden loss of support. Hence with downwardness the ideas of emptiness and chaos are likely to be associated. In the greater symbolic manifestations—i.e., those that have been religiously and dramatically most effective in their impact upon men—*up* and *down* do not stand alone, but are blended with certain other related ideas and images: notably, with the fiery light of divine wisdom, and with the fiery chaotic darkness of anguish, loss, and punishment.

But there is also a second symbolic meaning associated with downwardness—one which has left fewer traces in colloquial phraseology, but which has played a far larger role in mythopoeic thought. For *down* points toward the broad-bosomed earth, the ultimate mother and nurse of all living things. The *up-down* contrast, when it takes the more concrete form of a sky-earth relation, lends itself to ready personification, and thereby tends to become what will be defined in the next chapter as a "mythoid."

The archetypal symbol *blood* is capable of an unusually tensive and paradoxical character. Its full semantic range comprises elements of both good and evil, the former being fairly clear but the latter relatively obscure and all the more ominous for its obscurity. It is understandable that on the positive side "blood" should connote life, hence power in various forms, including the strength and dignity of inheritance, and that men from earliest known times should have employed red coloring agents in order to enhance a thing magically. But in most societies blood has a more ominous significance as well, which renders it taboo—that is, something to be dealt with ceremonially and on special occasions, not taken for granted and treated in a casual manner. Various explanations have been offered for the taboo character of blood. The most obvious is that since the spilling of too much blood produces death, blood becomes (whether avowedly or not) a death symbol. It is also connected with loss of virginity, and with female menstruation, both of which events usually have a taboo character among more primitive peoples. Moreover, by a natural logic blood becomes associated with the horrible penalties believed to be incurred by the violation of an oath: for when an oath is sworn by two or more contracting parties, it is usual for them to mix bloods and thus to become symbolically brothers,—an act which, on the supposition of firm brother-loyalty, makes the oath secure; a breaking of the oath is therefore a sullying of the common blood.

Since blood is associated with the moments of death, birth, puberty, the physical aspect of marriage, and war, as well as with the more general ideas of the health and strength (in special cases the pollution) of tribal life, it is very nearly co-terminous with that range of primitive ideas and rituals which van Gennep has called "rites of passage" (*rites de passage*).[1] According to van Gennep's well documented theory, every great event in tribal and individual life (at a time when the two aspects were not clearly distinguished) is regarded as a transition from one state of being to another, as a simultaneous death and rebirth in some respect. Such transitional events in tribal experience have to be met

ceremonially; and such ceremonies are at once magical
(in so far as they assist the event, help to push it to
fulfillment) and mimetic (in so far as they simply re-
assert in human terms—by dance, song, and image—
what the event intrinsically *is*). Magic and mimesis are
not actually separable at a primitive level, but it is
the latter aspect, rather than the former, that is of
direct importance for an understanding of symbols.

There is, to be sure, quite a diversity of images and
artifacts associated with transitional activities; but
functional congruities can often be discovered among
the differences. Pipe smoking, the phallus, and the
ploughing of fields seem to be three widely different
image-ideas; but each of them for its own set of reasons
tends to become a symbolic vehicle for major transitional activities. Among the North American Indians,
where pipe smoking was common, the action could
connote simultaneously the transitions from peace to
war and from war to peace, from life to death and (in
the case of childbirth) from death to life, from disease
to health, from drought to rain, and from seed-planting
to harvest. The phallus, too, besides being a more universal symbol than pipe smoking, can participate in
virtually the same array of meanings. Its relation to
blood, potency, generation, and death need not be par-
ticularized. Its relation to vegetation and the growth of
crops is reinforced by a widespread readiness to see a
connection between sexual union and the double act of
ploughing and seeding a field. Max Müller has traced
the philological connection between the *ar-* in "arable"

and the *er-* in *"eros"*—which he offers as one instance among many of how an ancient natural metaphor has become embodied and later stereotyped in language. Scattered confirmatory bits of evidence can sometimes be found in ancient literature. Creon in Sophocles' *Antigone*, when declaring that his son Haemon cannot marry the condemned Antigone, remarks cynically: "There are other fields in which he can push his plough." And a millennium earlier in Egypt the wise Ptah-Hotep had offered his celebrated advice to husbands: "Treat your wife with goodly devotion. She is a fertile field for her lord's ploughing."[2]

Of all archetypal symbols there is probably none more widespread and more immediately understandable than *light*, as symbolizing certain mental and spiritual qualities. Even in our current everyday vocabulary pertaining to mental phenomena there are many words and phrases that are products of earlier light metaphors: *elucidate, illuminate, clarify, illustrate, bright,* etc. On the whole these words have ceased to function as active metaphors and have lost all tensive character, becoming mere trade-words; it may be, however, that a more explicit phrase such as *throw light on* still retains some metaphoric life for those who employ it consciously.

The earliest known instance of the *light* symbol is found at Sippar in ancient Mesopotamia, toward the end of the third millennium B.C. On the fertile plain between the Tigris and Euphrates Rivers there flourished, some forty to forty-five centuries ago, the oldest school of which there is any record. Young men who

wished to learn would congregate from all over Mesopotamia, and perhaps from outlying regions too. Exca-
vations have shown that they sat on rude stone benches
without backs; and from what is known of that early
culture it may be presumed that their studies consisted
mainly of the art of cuneiform writing, medicine which
included magic, astronomy which was inseparable from
astrology, and the mythological and theogonic lore pertaining to their complex and often ambiguous pantheon.
Shortly before the Second World War an Oxford arche-
ological expedition discovered a buried stone on which
the antique characters could still be deciphered, and
which was judged to have served as lintel to the main
doorway of the school. The words which would thus
have greeted the student as he approached the entrance
to the building were these: *"May he who sits in the
places of learning shine like the sun!"*[3]

There are particularly three characteristics of light
that tend to suggest by analogy certain important
qualities of mind and spirit, for which the analogy of
light would therefore readily have come to mind as a
symbol. First and most evidently, light produces visi-
bility, it shows forth clear outlines which in darkness
vanish. By a natural and easy metaphoric step we can
pass from this observable action of light in the physical
world clarifying spatial boundaries and shapes to the
action of the mind bringing the boundaries and shapes
of ideas into intellectual configuration. Consequently
light readily becomes a sign of mental configuration—
which is to say, of mind in its most distinctive form.

In mythopoeic ages, however, light is not a visual

entity exclusively. Modern household appliances have so successfully enabled us to separate light and heat, that we are prone to forget how naturally in ancient times the two phenomena went together and hence how natural it was to think of them as two aspects of a single entity comprising them both as manifestations of itself. Even on a cold winter's day the sun could be felt in one's marrow. Consequently, in those contexts where light served as a symbol of intellectual clarity it tended to carry certain metaphoric connotations of fire as well. An important connotation in the history of symbolism is that which derives from the warming power of fire. As fire, glowing with light, warms the body, so intellectual light not only instructs but also stimulates the mind and spirit. The conception of intellectual light, as understood in earlier times, was likely to involve the warmth of enthusiasm not as a deliberate addition to its meaning but as a natural and inseparable aspect belonging to it.

Thirdly, there is a characteristic of physical fire that has always stirred men's imagination and challenged their powers of rational explanation: its power of seemingly spontaneous generation and rapid reproduction. From earliest times men have observed with awe that fire can often come into existence by sudden combustion and that it can increase in magnitude and intensity with dramatic quickness. In a more controlled fashion the flame could be multiplied from torch to torch and from hearth-fire to hearth-fire. Symbolically this suggested the aptitude of the mind to pass its light and heat, which is to say its wisdom and enthusiasm, along to other minds by quick contagion.

Along with these three major properties of fire that constitute the material basis of its symbolic importance there is also an important associated characteristic. Fire is widely, although not universally, connected in ancient times with the idea of *up*. Fire tends to fly upwards; moreover the ultimate source of earthly fire and light is the sun, who holds his daily place up there in the bright sky. The symbolical connotations of *up*, as has already been remarked, are prevailingly good; hence fire, too, usually has good connotations when it is associated with the idea of upwardness. In usual mythology the gods of light, or in monotheistic developments the God of Light, dwell in the bright sky, or else upon a high sacred mountain lighted by the sun's rays. Below lies the dark womb of Mother Earth; which, although opposed to the sky in some symbolical respects, need not be opposed axiologically, for the natural connotations of Mother Earth include not only corpses and ghosts but also the potentialities and furtherance of new life. Mythologically the effective opposite of any symbol is sometimes found to be rather different from what might logically have been expected.

Accordingly it becomes clear why ancient deities of light such as Ahura Mazda in Zoroastrian Iran, of fire such as Agni in Vedic India, and in general the gods who live "up there" in the bright sky, have frequently been described and addressed as possessors and sources of knowledge, particularly of moral knowledge. Ahura

Mazda is not only a powerful lord (*ahura*) and glowing (*mazda*) but also a wise one, as many hymns in
the *Zend Avesta* attest. Agni, "whose wealth is light,"
and who is the god especially associated with the sacred
domestic hearth-fire, is frequently addressed in the *Rig
Veda* as "knower" and "sage." Many other such examples could be found in different ancient religions;
and to a varying degree the same attitude has affected
the vocabularies of religions of the present day. Nevertheless it is well to avoid a too facile generalization; and
it should be noted that although a god of light does
tend as a general rule to be a god of knowledge as well,
the tendency is somewhat halted and modified by the
ways in which myths about the gods are developed.
Thus in India's Vedic period Dyaus, god of the bright
sky, does not appear to have been at all outstanding
in qualities of mind and spirit, whereas Varuna, god of
the encompassing sky and especially of the sky at night,
does have such qualities. For Varuna's moral wisdom,
his ability to look into the hearts of sinners, is associated with the fact that his worshipers can behold him
at night looking out of the black sky through his thousands of fiery eyes.

One further quality of light that has acquired symbolic importance is the tendency for excessive light to
produce a blinding effect, especially on weak eyes, and
thus to become associated with darkness. In the poetry
of Henry Vaughan, although eternity is "like a great
ring of pure and endless light," yet the poet represents
the mystery of encounter with Divinity as "a deep and

dazzling darkness." Scripture, too, employs this same theme of excessive light producing darkness. Although the Psalmist addresses God as one who covers himself "with light as with a garment," yet he also describes Him as "making darkness his secret place." The opposed conceptions receive a kind of logical reconciliation in a passage in the Epistle to Timothy, where Paul writes of God as dwelling in "unapproachable light, which no man has ever seen or can see." Light, for those incapable of beholding it, is darkness.

In many of the world's religions it is a frequent theme, although often without any hierarchic implications, that light and darkness are complementary and inseparable parts of the world-All. In the Oaxaca Museum there is a famous old Zapotec medallion, recovered from a tomb in Monte Alban. It is in the shape of a small disc, half gold and half silver, with a miraculously straight and fine line dividing the halves into two semi-circles. The traditional Yin-Yang symbol in China also involves the division of a disc into two equal halves, but the dividing line here is a snaky curve (a reverse S) and the suggested antithesis carries a number of merging connotations, the chief of which can be indicated in our language by the pairs *light-dark, male-female, life-death,* and *knowledge-ignorance.* The pipe of peace among the Plains Indians can be a pipe of war also, depending on the occasion when it is ritually smoked; for the puffs of smoke that are iconically associated with clouds, and hence signify rain and hence growth and plenty, can also suggest the gloomy overcasting of the sun and thereby the stern threat of war. The several paradoxes have obvious analogies with one another, and in the general history of symbolism the light-darkness antithesis tends to stand as a natural symbolic representative of the others.

The image of light is thus extraordinarily well fitted to stand as the principal imagistic symbol for mind; *light* is the semantic vehicle while *mind* is the tenor. The organic relationship between the two is expressed by an ancient Zoroastrian saying, preserved by Porphyrius: "The body of Ahura Mazda is light, his spirit is mind." The nature of mind is elusive and ambiguous, and no method of analysis can ever be adequate to a full understanding of it. But one thing we know about it indispensably—its power of discrimination. Whether in the field of action or in quiet contemplation the power to discriminate is the essential mark of mind, and this power above all is what *light* symbolizes.

When the Gathas of the *Zend Avesta* address the Deity as Ahura Mazda, "Lord Light," they make a compound symbol which is itself widespread enough to be called archetypal. A great lord, whether heavenly or earthly, is naturally bathed in light; and conversely light has a lordly character. The word "glory" preserves a record of the ancient readiness to associate the two ideas of lordship and light. Both the Latin *gloria* and the Greek Septuagint *doxa* are said to be translations of a Hebrew word that meant "intense light." Correspondingly the English word "glory," besides connoting, like the adjective "glorious," high nobility, also refers in an

iconographical context to an irradiation of light surrounding a group of religious figures—as distinct from
an aureole, which surrounds a single religious figure.
Light and glory, or light and lordship, have always
tended to enter readily into combination.

Light and lordship are two image-ideas drawn from
familiar experience which are elements in the complex
archetypal image-idea of Deity. "God is light, and in
Him is no darkness at all": this Scriptural statement
is one of the many Christian affirmations of light as a
symbol of divinity. In theology the image-idea of light
is developed into the abstract idea of omniscience, that
of lordship into the abstract idea of omnipotence. Although the ideas of omniscience and omnipotence are
humanly unintelligible and are probably both, when
examined in strict logic, self-contradictory, this slight
difficulty does not diminish their symbolic power. The
mythological ideas of light and lordship and the theological ideas of omniscience and omnipotence exercise
roughly parallel semantic functions.

The idea of lordship was closer to the idea of fatherhood in mythic ages than it is today, and the notion of
God as father, although not universal, is very widespread. Zeus was the father of a considerable number
of offspring, most of them illegitimate, and in general
his behavior as an archetypal parent was such as to
justify Aristotle's urbane remark, "It would be very odd
if anyone were to love Zeus." Nevertheless there were
shrines to Zeus in various parts of Greece, and there
were some who worshiped there. Philological evidence,

moreover, shows that his fatherhood was sometimes taken in a worshipful spirit. For there are pre-classical indications that the vocative form *Zeu peter* (Father Zeus, parallel to the Latin *Ju-piter* and the Sanskrit *Dyau-pitar*) had been employed in direct address. The notion of God as a severe but loving father in the Christian sense has not been held widely enough to be regarded as archetypal; but fatherhood in one way or another, and without any necessary implication of either moral or amiable characteristics, is an archetypal religious symbol.

Somewhat generally associated with this group of religious symbols is the further archetypal symbol, the Word. Man is by nature both speaker and spoken to; as he becomes more reflective the dialogue becomes internal and silent, but none the less real for that. The sense of being addressed—not by a hallucinatory voice, but by the silent voice which murmurs in some secret place beyond the inner ear—is felt in one way or another by every person of moral sensitivity. It is the something beyond impulse that can, on occasion, countermand and steer impulse. Thus the word, the Logos, tends to become an auditory image symbolizing rightness, the What Ought, which gives meaning to moral judgment. At a primitive level the divine command finds symbolization in certain physical noises: the rushing wind serves frequently as such a symbol, and the so-called bull-roarer, which imitates the wind's tone, is used by some American Indian tribes and elsewhere, to mime the supernatural voice and magically to invite and encourage it. Naturally and frequently the thunderbolt is taken as an audible manifestation and representation of the divine command. As religions become more developed spiritually such outward noises cease to matter, but the auditory image-symbol of Logos persists, as is shown in such a phrase as "the voice of conscience" and in such a word as "vocation."

Water as an archetypal symbol draws its universality of appeal from the combined properties of being a cleansing agent and a sustainer of life. Thereby water comes to symbolize both purity and new life, and in the Christian sacrament of baptism the two ideas are joined: the ceremonial water at once symbolically washes away the grime of inherited sin and also symbolizes the new spiritual life that is to be entered into. The latter aspect is particularly suggested by such phrases as "the water of life," by Jesus' dialogue with the Samaritan woman at the well (John iv), and by the scene in the uncanonical Gospel according to the Hebrews, in which the Holy Spirit descends not in the form of a dove, but as a fountain of water. Outside of Christianity any number of analogous instances of water symbolism are easy to find.

Perhaps the most philosophically mature of the great archetypal symbols is the Circle, together with its most frequent imagistic concretion the Wheel. From earliest recorded times the circle has been widely recognized as the most perfect of figures, both because of its simple formal perfection and for the reason stated in Heraclitus' aphorism, "In the circle the beginning and the end are the same."[4] When the circle is concretized as a wheel, two additional properties come in: the wheel has spokes, and it rotates. The spokes of the wheel are taken as iconically symbolic of the sun's rays; both the spokes and the rays being symbolic of the creative influences going out to all things in the universe from a central life-giving source. In its rotation a wheel has the property that when its axis is at rest the movement of its spokes and rim is perfectly regular—a property which readily becomes symbolic of the human truth that to find the quiet center of one's own soul is to produce a more tranquil ordering of one's experiences and activities.

Like many another archetypal symbol the Wheel is potentially ambivalent. It may have either a positive or a negative significance, and occasionally both. Negatively the Wheel can symbolize in the West the hazardous play of fortune, and in the East the persistent cycle of deaths and rebirths from which release is sought. Yoga, to the Hindu, is the patient disciplined exercise of action and non-action whereby an individual may prepare himself for such release. On the positive side, in addition to the symbolic import mentioned in the foregoing paragraph, the Wheel is in Hindu tradition connected with *Dharma,* or divine law. Buddhist iconography makes much of "the Wheel of the Law," and there is a widespread legend that Buddha, when he gave his first sermon after his initiatory vision under the *bo* tree (the so-called Deer Park Sermon), set it revolving. In traditional Chinese Buddhist ritual a chariot wheel is often fastened to a post and turned to the right, which is supposed to reflect the sun in its orbit and to symbolize the path of universal *Tao*. In Tibet the idea of the perfection and sincerity of universal law can be symbolized by so simple a gesture as joining the thumb with the middle finger. The Tibetan prayer wheel had originally the same meaning, and perhaps still retains it for informed worshipers, despite the crude magical uses to which it has later been put.[5]

A special development of the Wheel symbolism is found in the Buddhist tendency to let the purity of the still center be symbolized by the lotus flower. Reciprocally the wheel is often pictured as having a lotus at its axis and the lotus is often displayed with outgoing rays of light. The actual lotus flower has two characteristics that have especially struck the Oriental imagination—its simple pure beauty and its mysterious birth by water. A Buddhist teaching says that as the lotus flower arises from the dark depths of the lake to reveal itself in beauty, and as the sun arises in darkness and sends forth his rays, so Buddha issues forth from "the dark womb of being" in order to chase away the darkness of illusion (*maya*) by revealing the truth. In India the wheel is sometimes laid on the top of a pillar, as an icon of the lotus in full bloom on its stem. In the widely revered *Lotus Scripture* of Mahayana Buddhism the principal teaching is at once the eternity of divine law and the multiplicity of ways of expressing and teaching it—the still center and the many spokes or rays of the divine sun-wheel.[6]

The symbols that have been adduced as instances are

all familiar enough; what is here desirable is to see them as extensions and stabilizations of metaphorical activity. Thought is not possible to any significant degree without language, nor language without metaphoric activity whether open or concealed; the stabilization of certain metaphors into tensive symbols is a natural phase of the process. While any given symbol— the Cross, or the Flag, or the Divine Father, or the act of genuflection—can be examined sceptically and can be rejected as outworn, or as superfluous, or as involving ideas and attitudes to which the critic is antipathetic, a rejection of all symbols would be, in the last resort, a rejection of language and thought themselves. When a straightforward thinker sets out to free himself from symbolic and metaphorical thinking, what he actually means to do is limit himself to those symbols and rigidified metaphors which have become habitual stereotypes in everyday life. The issue is not between symbolic and non-symbolic thinking, but between limiting one's thought and sensitivities to the plain meanings denoted by conventional symbols and learning to think with a more tensive alertness. "The Lord whose oracle is at Delphi," said Heraclitus, "neither speaks nor conceals, he gives signs." Tensive symbols may perhaps offer hints about the nature of things which straightforward techniques must either ignore or distort. If reality is largely fluid and half-paradoxical, steel nets are not the best instruments for taking samples of it.

SEVEN

On the Verge of Myth

O F PARTICULAR INTEREST for an understanding
of literature, religious belief, and human culture generally, are the varied and often obscure causal
relations that have existed between tensive language
and the emergence of myth. Of course there are non-
linguistic causal factors as well. Among the principal
ingredients of myth must be counted ritual practices,
curiosity about nature, a vague but powerful sense of
presence lurking within or amidst or behind everyday
objects, a developing moral sensitivity that seeks outward justification, and together with all these a readi-

ness to believe that what is seen and enacted here in earthly existence is somehow copied after a nobler model or is following out some original divine command. These ingredients overlap, their individual working is not always evident, and no doubt the list could be extended. As a matter of fact there must be added the sheer love of story-telling, which produces the fanciful elaborations which are a large part of any developed myth. But of course fanciful stories by themselves do not constitute myth. What distinguishes a myth from a folk-tale is indicated by the final phrase in Alan Watts' definition: "Myth is to be defined as a complex of stories—some no doubt fact, and some fantasy—which, for various reasons, human beings regard as demonstrations of the inner meaning of the universe and of human life."[1] Attempts to express and justify the inner meaning of What Is are notoriously difficult, and a principal key to the difficulty—the difficulty of a finite creature trying somehow to grasp and speak forth the infinite—is to be found in the vagaries of man's language. For language is concerned, at its best, with trying to say What Is, and the attempt is always doomed either to fragmentation (as when the problem of reality is formulated in steno-terms and handed over to technical methods) or to partial frustration and vagueness. But the doom is not complete; for by imaginative language some inroad, genuine though slight, can be made into the semantic wilderness. Since imaginative language is basically metaphoric (in the sense that has been developed in earlier chapters) there is a natural collusion between metaphor and myth in man's attempts to discover and utter "the inner meaning of the universe and of human life."

The subject of myth should, of course, be studied with as non-partisan an attitude as possible, without falling into either of two kinds of easy prejudice regarding it. There is the creedal prejudice on the one hand, that some particular set of mythic beliefs, such as those of Christian orthodoxy, are true while all others are either false or at best approximations or distortions; and there is the positivistic prejudice on the other hand, that all mythic beliefs whatever, Christian or pagan, ancient or modern, sky-oriented or earth-oriented, are equally false. Suppose that a comparative view is taken, for example, of the tale told in the Gospels of Matthew and Luke of the virgin birth of Jesus and the tale told in the Buddhist birth narratives of the descent of the Buddha's spirit into the maternal womb in the form of a baby elephant. Orthodox Christians will accept the first of these tales as historically true and dismiss the second as false and fanciful; positivists will dismiss both narratives alike. Now clearly, there is an observable analogy between the two narrative traditions. Both of them deal with miraculous events attending the birth of a uniquely exalted spiritual teacher. It is possible therefore, and it may be enlightening, to adopt a perspective which considers the two sets of tales as similar in kind; and it should be possible to speak of this similarity, and to classify the tales according to it, without making prejudicial assumptions as to historical truth or falsity. The most objective method, and intellectually the most fruitful, is to bracket off the question of historical truth or falsity—that is, to put it aside as unanswerable and irrelevant—and to concentrate upon the characteristics of the two ancient narratives as related to man's central and always partly frustrated endeavor to say What Is. In order to avoid the implication of falsity that is attached in many people's minds to the words "myth" and "mythical," there is reason to prefer the neutral noun *mythos* and the neutral adjective *mythic*. The latter word will regularly be employed in the discussion that follows; the former, however, sounds rather too heavy and unnatural, and so it will have to be remembered that the word "myth," when it occurs, is here employed in its affirmative and contentual rather than in its negative and pejorative sense.

Alan Watts' definition, quoted above, has both the negative advantage of avoiding any connotation of "untrue" or "unhistorical" as a part of the word's meaning, and the double positive advantage of stressing both the narrative character and the transcendental reference of myth. To be sure, whenever the question is raised concerning what myth "is," there is danger of confusing matters of fact with strategies of definition. While truth is terminally more important than its agencies of expression, the purpose of a good definition is to dispel, if possible, a few of the clouds that veil it. An accurate definition is never final, but it is a help in getting started. Now despite the valuable contributions of Ernst Cassirer to mythic studies, I think we are obliged to regard as inadequate—valuably one-sided but still inadequate—his neo-Kantian, epistemological interpretation of myth. For myth, in Cassirer's definition, is taken as synonymous with the mythopoeic mode of consciousness—a view that has also found expression in Susanne Langer's treatment of myth as a primary type of human expression, parallel to, but distinct from, the other primary types, language, religion, and art.[2] Now it is true, and in fact is an indispensable part of the present thesis, that myth does involve a mode of awareness, and if that primary epistemological aspect is ignored there is a tendency to confuse myth either with folklore on the one hand or with ideology on the other. The mythopoeic imagination has indeed been an essential and primary factor in the formation of myths, and perhaps a part of the reason for our spiritual impoverishment under the conditions of modern living is the difficulty, amid these conditions, of rejuvenating the mythopoeic imagination and taking it seriously. But while it is true that myth is primarily centered in a mythopoeic outlook, it characteristically involves expressions of that outlook in the form of particular, concrete narratives. A myth not only expresses the inner meaning of things; it does this, specifically, by telling a story.

However, the most interesting thing about myths (when we have passed beyond the perspective of childhood) is not the stories in themselves, shaped as they have been by popular fancy through much telling and re-telling, but rather the interplay of human thought, feeling, imagination, and language (the four factors being by no means clearly separable) that appear to have contributed to the early stages of mythic formation. Such an inquiry into obscure origins, both psychological and anthropological, can only be plausible at best; nevertheless if the evidence is drawn from careful comparisons of linguistic, imagistic, and mythological materials, the plausibility may sometimes be fairly strong.

From the cumulative evidence of ancient literary remains a general negative conclusion can be accepted as true without serious dispute: namely, that early man, unlike ourselves, did not dichotomize his world into a law-abiding physical universe on the one hand and a confused overflow of subjective ideas on the other. Nature and self, reality and fancy, for him were radically interpenetrative and coalescent. The nearest he came to envisaging his world dualistically was, as Cassirer has remarked, to distinguish between the sacred and the secular. But the distinction was largely fluid and shifting, except where it might become stabilized by definite rituals, taboos, stories, and priestly authority. Nevertheless, in this fluid and ready interplay between the secular and the sacred, the latter must have been an ever-present reality, with indefinite powers of blessing and bane. Probably an outstanding and frequently recurring fact about an early man's world-as-experienced (for the world and the experience were not conceived as two) was his sense of a hovering, latent presence or presences within, amidst, or behind the familiar things that surrounded him. His world, we may say, was *presential*. By this word I mean something fairly close to what Rudolph Otto has called "the numinous."[3] The word "presential" has the advantage, however, of avoiding specifically religious connotations, although by no means excluding them; it will therefore be better suited to describe that quality of the world which the primitive myth-maker, the man of religious sensitivity, and the developed poetic consciousness all have in common.

Presential Reality and Metaphor

BOTH epiphoric and diaphoric activities show themselves in early developments of symbol and myth. Epiphor shows itself wherever man sees through the immediate to some lurking, perhaps some "higher" reality, in any case some meaning that transcends the sense of the epiphoric vehicle. When Philemon and Baucis discover their visitors to be gods, or when Aeneas discovers that the huntress with whom he has been conversing on the way to Carthage is his goddess mother, the scenic representation in each case gives an indication (charmingly light in Ovid's tale, seriously engaging but momentary in Vergil's) of how readily, to the ancient mind, a quite ordinary-looking person might reveal himself as a numinous presence.[4] Totemism represents an analogous proneness on the part of animals to become something more than meets the eye—a proneness that becomes regulated and formalized in those societies where totemism is accepted as an institution. Sacred places, too, may be presential epiphorically. Imagine the experience of a primitive woman who discovers herself pregnant, in a society where the cause of pregnancy is not understood, and who makes this discovery while she is passing through a certain grove. To her mind, which does not make the conventional modern distinction between subject and object, the grove suddenly becomes vibrant with meaning; in her emotional condition she probably communicates excitedly to her fellow-tribespeople what she has discovered about the grove, and as a result the grove is regarded thenceforth as sacred and taboo. In our own more technical vocabulary the grove becomes an epiphoric vehicle, of which the tenor is a daemonic force or local deity that has, and may suddenly exercise, the power of creating life.

Thus there is a stage of human awareness before the explicit formulation of a myth, which strongly disposes the persons who share it to formulate and rationalize various experiences in descriptive and narrative accounts. That earliest stage of mythic growth may be called a *mythoid,* or (when the matter is more general and less definite) a mythoidal situation. A mythoid is an incipient myth; more exactly it is a problematical situation that may, as a story-teller's fancy begins to operate, develop into a myth—that is, into a tale involving certain other-worldly person-like beings, who move about, perhaps bestowing benefits or playing pranks, and whose activities somehow illustrate, though perhaps dimly, some aspect of the inner nature of the world. In anthropological terms, when animatism gives way to animism, the idea of *mana* being succeeded by the idea of separate spirits or *daemons,* this marks a development from mythoid to myth. The sense of presence is perhaps the most important factor in a mythoidal situation, since the person who experiences it feels thereby strongly and naturally disposed to personify and to narrate.

As contrasted with an epiphoric mythoid such as has just been examined, where the semantic movement is from an outward shape and color to a latent meaning, a diaphoric mythoid would involve a synthesis of two or more forms charged with presentness. It may be that a purely diaphoric mythoid cannot be found, for there must be an epiphoric sense of Beyond if a myth is to arise. But there are mythoids in which the diaphoric element is observable and strong. The triple symbolism of Woman, Cow, and Crescent Moon is a pattern that repeats itself in various cultures. Each of the three images is likened to each of the others by a particular characteristic (A and B both give milk, A and C have monthly periods, B and C wear horns) and to that extent their relations are epiphoric; but the total triadic grouping, when viewed in a single apperception by early man, is diaphoric. But although there are ancient evidences of the three terms entering into imagistic and briefly anecdotal relationship with each other, it was not usual for a full myth to arise involving all three. That is to say, the cow-woman-moon triad constitutes, in many ancient societies, an undeveloped diaphoric mythoid.

A diaphoric mythoid that has enjoyed somewhat fuller development into explicit myths may be found in the several characteristics of the Vedic god Agni. Being a god of fire, Agni possesses several distinct characteristics: he lights up the world, and is therefore god of wisdom; he burns, and is therefore a stern judge and punisher of wrongdoers; he receives sacred butter which is thrown into him on the hearth with a large sort of spoon, and he thereupon sizzles and sparkles in carrying the sacrifice up to the gods on high, for which reason he is described both as the messenger to the gods and as having a spoon-shaped mouth. These attributes of Agni are repeated over and over again in the *Rig-Veda,* and are accepted as mythic stereotypes in much ancient Hindu literature; their diaphoric combination enters readily into the Hindu religious tradition.

A balance between epiphoric and diaphoric aspects can be found in the mythoid of the ancient Egyptian scarab. In mundane actuality the scarab was a dung beetle indigenous to North Africa, which would lay its eggs in dung, then shape the dung into a ball and roll it along the ground to a suitable hatching place. When the eggs were hatched there appeared to the Egyptian observers (to whom the tiny eggs were invisible) to be a miraculous case of what we should call spontaneous generation. At the same time there was a memory of the spheroid being pushed along the ground by the beetle. What would this combination of phenomena—creative generation and moving sphere—suggest? Naturally, the sun. For he, the sun, by his warm rays is the primary source of life, and he too is rolled across the sky—possibly, indeed quite likely, by a divine invisible beetle, a glorious heavenly archetype of the little insects crawling upon the earth. In the Egyptian hieratic language the heavenly beetle is distinguished by a special ideogram, translated as "scarab"; it is pictured as golden, taking its color from the sun; and it is endowed with universal generative power, of which the miraculous potency of the earthly dung-beetle is but a feeble copy. Now generation becomes, in the religious context, regeneration; and the gold scarab is thus a symbol both of eternal life after death and of moral regeneration. The two aspects find symbolic expression in the ancient Egyptian practice of removing the heart of a dead man and replacing it in the process of mummification by a small gold scarab. The scarab here signifies especially the redemptive power of Osiris, who, along with other attributes, was the god of immortality and new life, whose name a dying man would reverently and penitentially invoke.

The myths growing out of such mythoidal situations as the foregoing were usually but half developed by the ancient Egyptians, who did not have the same aptitude for constructing well-rounded tales as the Greeks. From the representations found in the Pyramid Texts and the Egyptian Book of the Dead it appears that the sun was conceived variously and plurisignatively as a winged disc, as a scarab with wings up-raised, as a pellet which the evil serpent Apophis keeps trying to swallow, as the falcon-headed god Re (who is also Atum) in a boat with a pilot in the bow sounding the blue waters of the sky with a pole, and in other ways. In the ancient city of Heliopolis (to give it its usual Greek name) a more philosophical type of myth took form among the priests of the sun cult. There the sun was regarded as the visible manifestation of the invisible Atum-Re, at once the progenitor of the divine Ennead (the traditional nine primary gods) and the divine essence permeating them all. His self-existence, the uniquely held power of being dependent upon nothing and no one but himself, is expressed in two mythic formulations: that he produced the race of gods and the race of men by taking his organ in his own hand, and that he created his own name. In the mortuary texts that make up the Egyptian Book of the Dead his self-existent character is proclaimed in such phrases as: "I am Atum, I am Re. I am self-created, born of myself."[5]

In the Nahuatl culture of the ancient Aztec people a complex diversity of mythological lore surrounds the curious figure of the goddess Tlazolteotl. At first sight it appears baffling that a single goddess should be worshipped as a sort of Aztec Venus who stirs the fires of love, sometimes as the mother of the gods, and even as a redemptive goddess who has the power to cleanse a penitent worshiper of his sins; while at the same time she is feared as the deadly scorpion and is despised as the "eater of filth." How do these incongruous traits become attached to a single mythic personage? A little analysis makes the strange mythic diaphor more understandable. The basic pair of facts from which to start is that Tlazolteotl is an earth goddess and that her name is derived from an old Nahuatl word-root meaning "to burn." From these two apparently original characteristics the others emerge by a natural development.

Since the etymology of the goddess's name connotes burning, it is natural that she should have developed certain traits logically connected with that idea. Two such traits in particular appealed to the early Aztec imagination: the burning power of sensual love and the burning sting of the deadly scorpion. The need to rationalize this pair of divergent characteristics produced the following folktale. It was told that the goddess in her mundane life had a husband named Jappan, who was very boastful. One of his boasts was that he could remain chaste even with so passionate a wife as his. Such a boast was not pleasing to the gods, and they deployed the demon Yastl to spy upon the man and see that he kept his vow. One day while climbing over rocks with his wife Jappan heard her call for help, and going to her assistance he struggled to lift her over a high rock. She told him that the only way he could help her was by pushing her thighs. He did so, and she thereby attained the ledge; her husband, however, found his powers of resistance quite depleted, and he succumbed. When Yastl the spy reported the incident to the gods, they were angry with Jappan for being a

vain braggart and changed him into a scorpion, where-
upon he hid himself in shame under a stone. His wife
was then served in the same way, so that she, who
represented love's fires, now became "the burning one"
also in the less pleasant sense of possessing the scorpion's fiery sting.

But all the while Tlazolteotl is also an earth goddess.
Of course it is a general mythic archetype that a goddess of love should also be goddess of the fruitful, re-
productive earth, but while it is probable on general
comparative grounds that the goddess's function as
earth-mother developed from the idea of burning love
that was associated with her name, there is no specific
evidence for it. In any case, having become, by mythic
logic, the "eater" of everything that was cast into the
earth, she became in particular the eater of filth and
excrement. By an easy transition, then, she became the
remover of filth from body and soul alike (between
which the Aztecs did not pretend any clear distinction). Thus she became the "sin eater," and in that
capacity she would receive prayers from the penitent.
Being the destroyer of filth, both bodily and spiritual,
she therein became the Aztec goddess of redemption.[6]

The Role of Linguistic Accident

SINCE the mythopoeic imagination expresses itself
most fully and revealingly in the language of words and
syntax, it is sometimes the case that the development of
mythoid into myth is furthered by some misunderstand-

ing of what the words or the syntax, when they expressed the original mythic insight, were intended to mean. In short, some myths and some aspects of quite a few myths have developed out of a linguistic matrix. The leading philologist of the nineteenth century, Friedrich Max Müller, looked for linguistic explanations everywhere, even at length going so far as to characterize mythology in general as "a disease of language" and any particular myth as "a word which, from being a name or an attribute, has been allowed to assume a more substantial existence."[7] Most names of Greek, Roman, and Hindu gods, he maintains, represent developments of words which "were gradually allowed to assume divine personality never contemplated by the original inventors." Müller can point, truly enough, to various instances that support his theory—e.g., that the myth of Tithonus and Eos being husband and wife presumably arose from a metaphorical description of the relation between dawn (*eos*) and the dying day (*tithonos*). Much can be learned from exploring such etymological factors in myths when (as happens all too rarely) a sufficient knowledge of the relevant early language developments is available. But Müller unfortunately brought the sometimes promising theory into discredit by the uncritical zeal with which he overstated it. It is high time that the real though limited possibilities of the linguistic approach to myth should be examined in a more restrained way.

A more extended instance offered by Müller has to do with the probable origin of Hecate, dark goddess of the crossroads and of crimes committed by night. Quite evidently the Greek word "Hekate" would have been the feminine of "Hekatos," which would have meant "the far-reaching one" or "the far-darter," and thus would naturally have been used as an epithet for the sun. By usual mythic logic, then, the feminine word "Hekate" would have meant the moon. From this etymological evidence it is circumstantially probable that Hecate was in pre-classical times a moon goddess. On this hypothesis it would appear that in the passage from the archaic to the classical period two things occurred. First, the suppositious sun god, Hekatos, dropped out of the picture, for in surviving classical mythology there is no mention of him. Secondly, another word for the moon, "*selene*," became current, so that the word "Hekate" lost its original semantic function. As a result the goddess Hecate was left, as it were, a semantic widow. Three characteristics, however, she retained: she was feminine, she had supernatural powers inspiring awe, and she was somehow connected with the moon. To fit her into an available place, popular story-tellers and then mythologers began to conceive of her as goddess of the *dark* of the moon; hence of dark night; hence of "the place where three roads meet," which was where ghosts were believed to congregate and where black magic was practiced; of cypress trees, connoting death; and of black deeds practiced in darkness. In the last aspect she became patron goddess of robbers.

A briefer mythological episode that may likewise

have grown out of a linguistic confusion is the traditional Greek account of Cronus devouring his children.
Now Cronus (called Saturn in Rome) was the father
of Zeus, and the important relation between them was
that Zeus overthrew his father and castrated him—the
celestial upheaval presumably reflecting some corre-
sponding shift of power on earth. The episode of eating
his offspring is not a natural part of the main story; it
has an adventitious look, as if it might have been a later
accretion. Müller has proposed the hypothesis that the
Greeks may have confused the name of the god,
Kronos, with the word for time, *chronos*. The letters *K*
and *X* (guttural *ch*) are fairly close together in Greek;
and it is evident from Plato's etymological speculations
in the *Cratylus* how readily the Greek mind could take
rough similarities of sound as supposed clues to significant identities. There is no basis in scientific philology
for connecting *Kronos* and *chronos*, but that is beside the
point; the question is how the early Greeks might have
regarded them. There is a familiar metaphoric sense in
which it can truly be said that time devours all things,
persons, and events—the infinite multitude of its ontological children. It might perhaps have been the case
that the early Greeks, starting with the metaphor and
confusing *chronos* and *Kronos*, produced the tale of the
god Kronos devouring his children. The example is
speculative but suggestive.

Turning from the field of classical mythology to folk-
loristic and anthropological evidences, we find various
and sometimes amusing examples of mythoids based

upon linguistic accidents. A trivial one, which can be
called a mythoid only by analogy, since what it produced was not a myth but merely a local legend, is to
be found among the Iroquois Indians of New York
State. It is related by them, and apparently believed,
that a former chieftain of the Onondaga tribe, Dekan-
owidah by name, dug his own grave and buried himself. To an outsider the question naturally suggests
itself how so improbable a tale could have arisen. Re-
cently an anthropological observer, finding that the
legend is still told and believed among the surviving
remnants of the Onondaga tribe, sought out its origin
and discovered the following explanation.[8] It had been
the Iroquois custom that after a chieftain's death his
name should be passed on to his successor. But Dekan-
owidah, being a very proud man, issued an edict forbid-
ding that anyone else should take his name after his
death. The older Iroquois had described his action as
"burying himself." From the metaphor, after its meaning became tribally forgotten, the legend arose.

In Nahuatl mythology the Aztec god Tlaloc, traditionally painted black with a green helmet and white
feathers, was god of the waters. The Aztecs wished to
distinguish four categories of water, one good and three
bad. Not possessing a word for the abstract idea of
categories they spoke of four pitchers or jugs. And so
the myth arose that Tlaloc (whose name appears to
have meant "pulp of the earth") possesses four jugs of
water from which he sprinkles blessings or bane upon
the Aztec land—the jugs containing respectively water

that is pure and drinkable, watery dampness that produces spiders and causes blight, cold frost, and inundating floods.

Not only the mistaken meaning of a separate word but also the mistaken meaning of syntax and of word-compounding may sometimes give rise to a mythoid. An example is provided by ancient Mayan theology. As far back as is known the Mayan god Itzamua was lord of the sun and the moon, of day and night, light and darkness—in short, the supreme God of the ancient Mayan people. In order to remind themselves of his unity the Mayan worshipers added the syllable *hun* (one) together with the syllable *ab* (state of being, connoting firmness and self-subsistence). Then, in order to affirm his divinity, they added the syllable *ku*, which could mean both "divine" and "god," there being no clear distinction between adjective and noun in the Mayan language. "Hunab Ku" tended to break off from the parent word of which it had been a descriptive adjunct, and to become an epithet in its own right. Hunab Ku became half-personified—enough so that the question presented itself to the Mayan mind how Hunab Ku ("Hunab the god") was related to Itzamua. At this stage the relation between Hunab Ku and Itzamua is a mythoid; it constitutes a mythoidal situation. Not being skilled in metaphysics like the Hindus, the Mayans did not develop a theory of avatars. Instead, they contrived stories, in which Hunab Ku was represented as the father and Itzamua as the son.[9]

Tendencies of Personification

A SPECIAL, widespread kind of metaphoric action takes the form of personifying. In acknowledging this to be the case, however, we should avoid a common fallacy of interpretation. Primitive personification is not a deliberate and fanciful thing such as it is when a later poet, from playfulness or for the sake of enlivening his discourse, calls the moon a lady or speaks of Father Time. The primitive thinker, unlike ourselves, did not start from a known world of inanimate things and then pretend they were otherwise. He started with a world that was not clearly animate or inanimate but hovered between the two conditions, sometimes partaking more of the one and sometimes more of the other. His world was already potentially animate, in that the awesome emergence of living presences in his surroundings, whether in animals, in fetishes or in sacred places, whether in waking moments or in sleep, was an ever imminent possibility. Add to this that his language contained few if any abstract words; it was drawn from human affairs and hence whatever he might want to say about the world had to be said in words humanistically charged and with anthropomorphic overtones. The most universal illustration of this is the way in which the attempt to speak of one's soul, one's own personal existence, repeatedly found expression in some word denoting breath. What could be more natural, in an age when no independent word for soul or self existed, than to express the idea epiphorically by employing as vehicle the nearest and most intimate of concrete experiences—the experience of breathing? Lacking an idiom whereby to say "I am" the primitive man does the best he can by saying "I breathe." The Indo-European root of the Sanskrit *asmi,* which bears this meaning, has subsequently been developed into both the "is" and the "am" of the extremely irregular verb "to be." [10]

From a lost play of Aeschylus, *The Daughters of Danae,* the following fragment has been preserved:

The pure sky [Ouranos] desires to penetrate the earth, and the earth is filled with love so that she longs for blissful union with the sky. The rain falling from the beautiful sky [Ouranos] impregnates the earth, so that she gives birth to fodder and grain for flocks and men.[11]

By the time that Aeschylus was writing his dramas the art of poetic personification had become highly elaborated, and his personification of the sky as Ouranos (mythologically the grandfather of Zeus) was certainly deliberate. Nevertheless the passage reflects a type of utterance that had been current in an earlier mythopoeic period, in which no linguistic and hence no clearly conceptual distinction had yet been drawn between the physical sky and the divine personage Ouranos. The idea of impregnation as a means of declaring the effect of the rain upon the earth was, at the beginning, a quite natural epiphor, and the personification of sky and earth as male and female agents respectively was a part of the epiphoric situation. Euripides has preserved what had apparently once been another natural epiphor of the same general kind, although with a more implicit sexual import:

> Parched earth loves the rain;
> And high heaven, rain-filled,
> Loves to fall earthwards.[11]

The interrelated acts of personifying and mythologizing are sometimes furthered in a context of prayer. For in praying a worshiper speaks as if to a living presence in direct address, and by speaking to it he tends to conceive it in a certain way, as a semi-personal being who can hear and respond. Petitionary prayers show the process most clearly, because of their relatively cruder nature. There is something very down-to-earth about asking for favors, and the god of whom a request is made is bound to be, for the moment at least, decidedly anthropomorphic in character. Unfortunately he has too much the look of a cosmic trust fund banker.

A penitential prayer generally expresses a more admirable human attitude, and it tends to postulate a more maturely spiritual kind of deity as the "Thou" to whom the prayer is addressed. In the *Rig-Veda* it is Varuna to whom the penitential hymns are most frequently addressed. Being the god of the night sky, with his many thousands of eyes looking down through the darkness, he can see penetratingly into the hearts of sinners, and hence it is natural to address one's penitential confessions to him. In a group of verses distributed among three hymns, written by the same *rishi*-poet

and set together in the seventh book of the *Rig-Veda*, a
worshiper of Varuna (presumably the poet himself),
evidently afflicted with dropsy but much more terribly
with darkness of soul, speaks as follows:

> I do not wish, King Varuna
> To go down to the house of clay.
> Be gracious, mighty lord, and spare.
>
> Since like one tottering I move,
> O slinger, and with inflated skin,
> Be gracious, mighty lord, and spare.
>
> Somehow through weakness of my will
> I went astray, O shining one.
> Be gracious, mighty lord, and spare.
>
> Thirst found thy singer even when
> He in the midst of waters stood.
> Be gracious, mighty lord, and spare.[12]

If these verses are penitential and petitionary together,
at least the two verses that follow are of a more purely
penitential and spiritual kind:

> Varuna took on board with him Vasistha,
> Made him a *rishi* by his mighty working;
> On gladsome days the Wise One made him a
>   singer,
> As long as days, as long as dawns continue.
>
> But now what has become of this our friendship,
> When lovingly we used to walk together;
> When, sovereign Varuna, to thy lofty palace,
> Thy thousand-gated house I had admittance?

Where is the line between myth and truth in an utterance of such unquestionable sincerity clothed in mythological imagery? The question leads us on to the larger problem to which the foregoing discussions of metaphor, symbol, and myth have pointed: What is the nature of reality in so far as tensive language, by virtue of its metaphoric and mythopoeic power, succeeds in speaking it? This is the question, the poeto-ontological question, to which we must finally turn.

EIGHT

The Sense of Reality

MAN, to the extent that he is awake, has a persistent concern for What Is. Neither mind nor language can exist or be conceived entirely apart from the object, the Otherness, which the mind implicitly seeks and which the language problematically signifies. Conversely, any object, any aspect of What Is, can claim existence only in relation to a responsive mind and only through some kind of language. But while these three factors are ontologically inseparable in any situation that can be experienced or imagined, it is the linguistic factor that has occupied the forefront

153

of attention during the last five chapters. The other two factors were always latent, however, and on occasion they peered forth—as when it was found that authentic myth in its origin involves both responsive wonder on the part of the subject and some form of intense presentness on the part of the object. The task of the present final chapter is to consider somewhat more focally the characteristics of reality in so far as it is an object of tensive language and of the responsive wonder that expresses itself through such language. From this standpoint the principal characteristics of living reality appear to be three: it is presential and tensive; it is coalescent and interpenetrative; and it is perspectival and hence latent, revealing itself only partially, ambiguously, and through symbolic indirection.

REALITY IS PRESENTIAL

WE ARE so habituated nowadays to thinking of "the real world" in terms of moving things and the forces propelling them, that it is hard to find appropriate words for speaking about that sense of presence out of which all that is genuine in religion, myth, art, and philosophy has originally grown. Although men are never entirely without a sense of the presential, it may become weak through either outward distractions or intellectual artifacts, and as it becomes weakened our sense of reality itself becomes slack.

A person's sense of presence is likely to be most strongly marked and most incontestably evident in his relationship, at certain heightened moments, with another human person. This is as it should be, for an individual sinks into a deadening egoism (however much he may gild it with idealistic verbiage or mitigate it by outward acts) unless he occasionally exercises and stretches his ability to realize another person as an independent presence to whom homage is due, rather than as merely an interruption of continuity in his environment. To know someone as a presence instead of as a lump of matter or a set of processes, is to meet him with an open, listening, responsive attitude; it is to become a *thou* in the presence of his *I*-hood. Most of us become a *thou* only occasionally and imperfectly; but it is the ability to do so, and the occasional actualization of that ability, that gives us the sense of personal otherness and enables us most readily to recognize presence as an independent dimension of reality.

The sense of presence may be felt toward inanimate objects as well. There is a Zen Buddhist story of a student who asked his Japanese Zen teacher: "If the Buddha is more than Siddhartha Gotama, who lived many centuries ago, then tell me, please, what is the real nature of Buddha?" The teacher replied:

The blossoming branch of a plum tree.

The pupil supposed that the teacher had not heard his question, so he said: "What I asked, worthy Sir, and what I am eager to know is, What is Buddha?" The teacher replied:

> A pink fish with golden fins swimming idly through
> the blue sea.

The pupil, now somewhat confused, said, "Will not
your Reverence tell me what Buddha is?" The teacher
replied:

> The full moon cold and silent in the night sky,
> turning the dark meadow to silver.[1]

The meaning of the teacher's evasion is not hard to
fathom. He was evading merely an unreal conundrum,
and was urging his befogged pupil to open his eyes and
heart and mind to reality at any point and so become
more intensely aware of it. The blessed state of being
is not something abstract or remote or future; it is the
everyday world, or some aspect of it, seen and felt and
contemplated with a new awareness and receptivity.

In describing the sense of presence as an independent
dimension of reality I intend the descriptive word in a
precise sense. A dimension, properly speaking, is an
independent variable; the sense of presence can vary
quite independently of empirical circumstances. The
most common objects and everyday situations, as well
as the most unpromising human individuals, may reveal
sudden and astounding possibilities of presence when
they are ignited by a suitably responsive-imaginative
act. The hyphen is used intentionally; for a genuine
responsiveness is imaginative, and a genuine imagina-
tiveness is responsive. An authentic work of art touches
off such responsiveness in the beholder or listener, and

thereby reveals presence in freshly imaginative ways. In so doing the work of art functions metaphysically, and this is the only sense in which art has any right, *qua* art, to be metaphysical.

In the classical Chinese tradition the conceptual formulation is a little different. Perhaps because of the different, almost incommensurable semantic potencies of an ideogrammatic language the *I-thou* relationship is not so directly stated, but there is no great change of meaning when the stress is put upon "reciprocity." In that seventeenth century Chinese treatise on the art of painting, which goes by the name of *The Mustard Seed Garden Manual*,[2] there are not only rules for the mixing of paints and for the exorcism of hostile spirits from the painter's surroundings, there are also bits of advice about the right attitude for the painter to take toward his objects—with revealing implications as to what and how the objects, on their part, really are. When you paint a man looking at a mountain (so the instructions run) the man should be slightly bent in appropriate homage to so lordly a being; and the mountain, too, should seem to be bowing slightly and with permissive dignity toward the man. Similarly, when a lutist is plucking out music from his instrument under the moon, he should seem to be listening to the moon; while the moon in turn, cold and still, should appear to be listening to the lute player. Such appearances of reciprocity are essential to the art of *jên-wu* painting—which is to say, the painting of human figures in landscapes, or, by extension, the painting of landscapes which show, by means of such things as a little bridge or a bamboo hut, the effect of human art. Hence, whether the human figures are actually shown in the painting or not, the landscape tends to look presential, alive, and delicately responsive.

A presence is a mystery—not an enigma that arouses our curiosity, but a mystery that claims our awe. Every presence has an irreducible core of mystery, so long as it retains its presential character. Explanations, theories, and specific questionings are directed toward an object in its thinghood, not in its presentness. An object in its thinghood is characterized by spatio-temporal and causal relations to other objects in their thinghood: we inquire about its name, its place, its why and whither, its status according to some system of values. All such questions are peripheral. When, on the other hand, two persons meet and their meeting is one of mutual presentness, the essentiality of their meeting has nothing to do with names and addresses. If such information is exchanged, it is done either from convention or for practical reasons or in a spirit of play. The real awareness in a personal meeting is something quite other than informational detail. No multiplication of such details, however full and meticulous, can be a substitute for real meeting; often, indeed, the details may darken and blur the meeting by misleading the mind into side paths. The same is true when no other human being is involved, and hence no assured mutuality. The sense of presence that occurs to one who catches a sudden glimpse of, say, a certain contour of hills or of a red wheelbarrow in the rain, defies explanation; for when explanations are begun or sought the sheer presentness diminishes or disappears.

Psychologically, of course, there are always personal backgrounds which determine, or partially determine, why one person feels presence here, another there. The surface simplicity of a sense of presentness can be deceptive; for although the simplicity does exist in so far as an experience of it is had (by the nature of the case there cannot be any way of refuting that!), yet the peculiar character of this or that experienced simplicity has been made possible by an indeterminate network of psychic associations that is never the same in any two individuals. That is why simplicity cannot for the most part be conveyed simply. A classical case (and apparently a classical failure) of the attempt to convey a simple experience through sheer simplicity of statement is to be found in Section xxi of William Carlos Williams' *Spring and All*. The eight short lines of the section, although they bear no distinguishing title, form an independent unit with no imagistic or thematic outside connections, and it may therefore be treated (as its author has, in fact, publicly spoken of it) as a single poem. The statement runs:

> so much depends
> upon
>
> a red wheel
> barrow

glazed with rain
water

beside the white
chickens[3]

That is all. To most readers it will be accepted as a pleasant pastiche, with no more than a fanciful justification for the opening words. To Dr. Williams, however, as he has repeatedly declared, the small remembered scene is of arresting and retaining importance. But quite obviously the personal associations and bubbles of memory that have stirred the poet's sensitive recollections are not shared by a reader whose only clues are to be found in the poem itself. The trouble is that in these lines the poet has tried to convey the simplicity of the remembered experience by a plain simplicity of utterance—by a simple simplicity, one might say, as opposed to a contextual simplicity. The attempt was bound to fail. Simplicity, when it is fresh and not banal, can scarcely be conveyed to another mind, except in rare instances where, by happy accident, two diverse sensitivities happen to be attuned in just that respect. For more assured communication the poet must construct a *mimesis* of simplicity.

Since a poet cannot expect to be supplied with readers in such perfect attunement that his unspoken associations will go freely out to them, his job is in part to offer delicate suggestions whereby an appropriate response may perhaps, in the more alert minds, be awakened. Without some such quiet directedness there is

danger that readers, in giving context to the images
they receive, may, for want of clues, draw too much
upon their own subjective associations. Referring to her
line quoted in an earlier chapter, "Pigeons on the grass
alas," the late Gertrude Stein once declared in a radio
interview, "That is exactly how I felt about it." No
doubt. But the intensity of the experience that the
poetess remembered as lying beneath the words is not
to be communicated by simply repeating the simple
phrase. "A rose is a rose is a rose" does nothing whatever to convey to anyone else Miss Stein's probably
lively feelings about roses. A sense of presence cannot
be communicated by simple statement, inasmuch as the
associations that connect the statement with the experience of one person are unlikely to be available, except
by miracle, to another.

What the red wheelbarrow poem lacks, what Stein's
roses lack, and what a successful imagist poem needs
to have, is a more tensive presentation. Why? Because
when two imagistic elements are put in a tensive relation to each other a slight pattern is established—a
flexible, unobtrusive pattern—and this is something
that can be communicated. Analogously, and appealing
to a more naked form of sense-impression, two persons
cannot be sure, when both are looking at a red surface,
that their experience of color-tone is the same; on the
other hand, when each observes the other arranging
shades of red in the same way as himself and distinguishing them from blues, there is objective assurance
that the *patterns* of experience are virtually the same.

When an imagist poem is successful in communicating not merely its visual imagery but also its full mood—its shy ontological claim—to the reader, the success is made possible by some diaphoric, tensive collocation of elements. There is no such collocation in Stein's tautology of the rose, which accordingly does not communicate. Williams, by contrast, can expand an initial tautology into variegated significance, as he has done in "Primrose":

> Yellow, yellow, yellow, yellow!
> It is not a color.
> It is summer!
> It is the wind on a willow,
> the lap of waves, the shadow
> under a bush, a bird, a bluebird,
> three herons, a dead hawk
> rotting on a pole—
> Clear yellow! . . .[4]

What does this passage do that the wheelbarrow description fails to do? Instead of presenting a single scene and staking everything on the improbable hope that a reader may succeed in feeling about it as the poet does, the present passage offers a succession of precise visual images, returning at last to the color-image from which it started. Thus the relevant significance of "yellow" becomes built up by associations within the poem, instead of by private associations locked in the poet's head.

Many of the poems in *Spring and All* achieve a more authentic objectivity, a surer communicability of sentiment, than the lines about the red wheelbarrow; and they do this usually by bringing together images that at once stir contrasting moods and, as a complementary aspect of the same semantic act, evoke reality in different individual guises.

> By the road to the contagious hospital
> under a surge of the blue
> mottled clouds driven from the
> northeast—a cold wind.
>
> Pink confused with white
> flowers and flowers reversed
> take and spill the shaded flame
>
> Crustaceous
> wedge
> of sweaty kitchens
> on rocks
> overlapping
> thrusts of the sea
>
> The decay of cathedrals
> is efflorescent
>
> The veritable night
> of wires and stars

In another idiom there comes the presential quality of Edwin Muir's "The Wayside Station," which begins:

> Here at the wayside station, as many a morning,
> I watch the smoke torn from the fumy engine
> Crawling across the field in serpent sorrow.

> Flat in the east, held down by stolid clouds,
> The struggling day is born and shines already
> On its warm hearth far off. . . .[5]

The presented sense of actuality is not without suggestions of tensive contrast, but these are subdued and are always subordinate to the totally imagined scene. Stephen Spender has praised the poem "because it expresses so exactly an experience and a sequence of thought which is the rhythm of the eye, the ear and the mind." It is in this sense that effective presentation and appropriate tension are inseparable.

REALITY IS COALESCENT

To ENVISAGE sharp lines is a subterfuge of thought, which is constantly trying to veer off along tangents of its own making. Some of these intellectual demarcations become respectable by repetition, or perhaps serve a useful purpose in marking off areas for attention and research. The most insistent of them in our time is the Cartesian dichotomy, the glib dualism between mind and matter, or (in a slightly different perspective) between subject and object. The utilities of the situation are found in the need of clarifying the subject-matter of scientific investigation. Such clarification is necessary to be sure, but it does not, if rightly understood, necessitate a dualism. Out of the infinitude of What Is—the infinitude of actual and potential experience—it is always possible, and sometimes desirable, to limit one's attention to one set of characteristics, systematically ignoring all other kinds. Some such intellectual selectivity is required in any focussed enterprise. The concept of the physical universe which has been found workable by modern physical science since the Renaissance is a product of the most concerted and consistently developed process of intellectual selection. The qualitatively blended world of Anaxagoras, the Hindu world of luxuriant illusion, the prevailing colors and forms that make up the visual world of Cezanne— each of these has involved its own kind of serious selection. But in each case the vogue is more limited, and by our present standards of utility the perspective that is involved is likely to seem somewhat odd and unsubstantial. To the down-to-earth, positivistic mentality of our day such notions of reality as are implicit in a Cezanne painting will seem to be invalidated by their perverse and annoyingly infirm conception of what's what—by an unclear distinction between what is really so and what isn't. There is no widespread temptation to construct a metaphysical dualism out of the kind of attention that a painter's eye and brush demand. Such a temptation comes rather out of the unexamined implications of familiar speech and familiar ways of making associations. It has become a commonplace of modern thought to take certain characteristics of a thing, such as the distance and size of the sun, as "objectively real" and certain other characteristics, such as the sun's grandeur and even (by the strict implications of Cartesian theory) its yellowness, as "merely subjective";[6] and to dichotomize the totality of possible experiences into what is and what is not of a sort to be conceptualized by the methods and language of science.

The trouble with making an intellectual cleavage between subjective mind and objective matter is twofold: it gives undue prestige to certain aspects of experience (those which we call collectively the "physical" aspects) at the expense of other and perhaps intrinsically more important aspects; moreover it generates artificial questions. To ask (as philosophical aestheticians often do) whether the beauty of a rose is in the rose or in the eye and mind of the beholder is palpably an unreal question, for the correct answer is "Both;" and if the answer looks contradictory, so much the worse for the dualistic structure of thought that makes it look so. The *I* who am aware and the *that* of which I am aware are but two aspects of a single sure actuality, as inseparable as the convex and concave aspects of a single geometrical curve. They can be distinguished intellectually, for the simple reason that they vary in their respective degrees of prominence in different situations. On one occasion the significant thing is the sensuous vitality which I imaginatively behold in a landscape and perhaps try to express with brush and paints; on another occasion the significant thing is that the landscape is dying an autumn death whether my subjectivity likes it or not. The role of the subject is somewhat weightier in the first situation, the role of the object in the second; but both subject and object are present as complementary aspects of every possible situation, however much the emphasis and the proportion might shift. Reality, as distinguished from the intellectual artifacts that often usurp the name, is neither object nor subject, neither matter nor mind, nor can it be limited to any other philosophical category; it is That to which every such category tries to refer and which every philosophical statement tries to describe, always from an intellectual point of view and always with ultimate inadequacy.

But when this much has been said a qualification must be made. For what is the *I* that seeks thus to coalesce with its world? Without attempting to define the *I* in a philosophically adequate manner (an attempt that would appear somewhat naive after twenty-five centuries of the most varied failures) we may at least observe that the poetically significant *I*—the *I* as it enters into the making and into the appropriate reception of a poem—consists largely of images, visual, auditory, motor, and structural. Such images are always particular in their existence, but in their intent they are more than particular, for they point and hint and inquire indefinitely beyond. Thus the first kind of coalescence, between self and not-self, involves a second kind between particular and universal.

To the poetical mode of awareness the particular, without losing any of its bright actuality, tends also to be, or at least to suggest overtones of, something more. In another place I have argued [7] that when Heraclitus speaks of "fire" as the primal constituent of reality, he does not mean merely the physical phenomenon that shines and scorches, nor does he mean merely the universal fact of unceasing process; he means both. A clear distinction between particular and universal, which seems so natural and easy and right to any practiced thinker today, is not found at the early stages of civilization; it is a product of later, more sophisticated thought and of closer attention to the implications of grammar. Abstract universals are a product of logical analysis; in Greece an understanding of them was of slow growth, resulting from the successive contributions of (in the main) Parmenides, Socrates, Plato, and Aristotle. Concrete universals, on the other hand—in which the particular actuality is one with all other things of the same species—are the natural and usual terms of thought in a pre-sophisticated civilization, and they persist in, or at least leave their traces on, the poetic mode of thinking in times thereafter. Plato, who in the Dialogues of his middle period manages to combine the poetic and the logical mode of thinking in so distinctive a manner, recognizes the fact of coalescence between particulars and universals. For a particular exists, according to his teaching, by participation (*methexis*) in the universal reality that gives it its main significance, and conversely the universal reality permeates all particular things to different degrees, much as the pure light of the sun illuminates the different objects of a landscape to different degrees, each according to its capacity for receiving. Particular things bulge with significance, to whatever extent they participate in, coalesce with, a something more that is consubstantial with themselves.

Coalescence takes place in the time-dimension as well; it appears therein as the phenomenon of radical change. To describe the changing character of things as "radical" is to accept, with Heraclitus and Aristotle, the testimony of experience that there is a genuine coming-to-be and passing-away; it is to reject the thesis of Parmenides and of the later Plato that the changing character of things is merely delusive appearance or at most an inferior, second-class sort of being. The notion of permanent entities that stay absolutely the same and merely undergo redistribution to produce changing appearances is an intellectual fiction. Taking experience as it comes, instead of as it can be rationalized, what we obviously discover is that while some things change rapidly and others with laborious slowness, nothing whatever escapes metamorphosis. In her penetrating study of the role of metamorphosis in modern poetry[8] Sister Bernetta defends the thesis that the metamorphic mode, while most strikingly exemplified in the major poets of our time, is characteristic of poetic creation generally. If this is so, and if by our earlier postulation we recognize a continuity between the poem and the world that it describes and evokes, then it follows that metamorphosis, the continual passing of one qualitative state into another, is a primary ontological fact. The poem in its creativity expresses a representative character; it not only invents, but in its invention it obliquely records something of a metamorphic character in the world which it salutes.

REALITY IS PERSPECTIVAL

THE TWO foregoing characteristics of reality as envisaged through the medium of poetry and the poetic consciousness—both its presential and its coalescent aspects—make it impossible to postulate a single type of reality as ultimate. The communication of presential and coalescent reality is not possible by relying on words with inflexible meanings; if it is to be achieved at all (and the achievement is always imperfect at best) the common words must be chosen and contextualized with discriminating suitability. Much of the context is constructed in the act and by the manner of saying forth; it is not all previously given. The fresh context may be regarded as an angle of vision, a perspective, through which reality can be beheld in a certain way, a unique way, not entirely commensurate with any other way. A genuine perspective must partly create, justify and interpret the language by which it finds expression; therefore no such perspective can be reduced to another. To think or speak about reality is always to do so through one perspective rather than another, and to compare one perspective with another must involve the adoption of a third perspective which will be only partly pervious to them both. Thus reality as a whole cannot be typed, for to type it is to limit it to an arbitrarily chosen perspective. Anything that can be typed—whether electrons, or elements of logical discourse, or historical events, or minds as we understand and classify them, or religious figures as we imagine and talk about them—thereby (i.e., by the very virtue of being something rather than something else) shows forth its own ontological limits.

If we are willing to seek philosophical insights in and through the testimony of poetic diction and artistic forms, examining and responding to such insights in their fullness as they are presented—then a kind of basic, irreducible pluralism results. A reader may strongly feel a large truth-claim in *The Brothers Karamazov*, in *Hamlet*, in *A la recherche d'un temps perdu*, in *The Castle*, or in *Wozzeck*; but can he, or would he wish or dare to try to, fit their several truth-claims into a total system? The reason for the impossibility is plain. To systematize individuals is to relate and distinguish them on the basis of partial aspects that can be compared; but a whole work of literature, like a human individual, is not a totality of its partial aspects. To enter into the Karamazov "world" is one thing, and to enter into the Proustian "world" is another. The two worlds are not planets in a solar system that can be geometrically plotted; they are full individual experiences, each of them offering independent possibilities, on its own terms, of a continuing something more. The reality that is discovered through the experience of reading one of these novels is different in kind from a reality that is discovered by means either of microscopes or of statistical curves, and different again from the reality that may be encountered in a rough adventure, or again from that which may be found in prayerful communion. It is only by an arbitrary limitation of the word "reality" that the claims of one kind of experience can be called "real" and those of other kinds "unreal." But to limit the word is to evade the problem. For the problem of reality is man's ultimate problem; his judgment, "Such-or-such is more real, or more

deeply real, than something else," is a major expression
of his intellectual faith. In order to exercise his basic
intellectual rights he must be allowed at least this one
word, the predicate "real," by which to mark his most
responsible ulterior judgments.

From the contextual and perspectival character of
reality it follows that the nature of reality is intrinsically
and ultimately hidden from any finite exploration.
When Heraclitus declared that "Nature loves to hide"
and that "The Lord whose oracle is at Delphi neither
speaks nor conceals, but gives signs," he was indicating
a fundamental and permanent characteristic of What
Is, and not a temporary state which man's increasing
knowledge would some day succeed in rectifying. Reality is ultimately problematical, not contingently so; for
to grasp and formulate it, even as a set of questions, is to
fragmentize it. There is always, in any inquiry, something more than meets the eye, even the inner eye; the
permanent possibility of extending one's imaginative
awareness has no limits. A person of intellectual sensitivity is plagued by the sense of a perpetual Something
More beyond anything that is actually known or conceived. A wise beginning for any large inquiry is to
entertain the postulate that reality, or a goodly part of
it, is not obvious and discoverable by overt public
methods of investigation, but is latent, subtle, and shy.

If reality is intrinsically latent and unwilling to give
up its innermost secrets even to the most enterprising
explorer, then the best we can hope to do is catch
partisan glimpses, reasonably diversified, all of them

imperfect, but some more suited to one occasion and need, others to another. If we cannot hope ever to be perfectly right, we can perhaps find both enlightenment and refreshment by changing, from time to time, our ways of being wrong. All human resources may usefully be tapped, and most particularly the products of man's creative activity. The mythic and the fictive should not be dismissed from consideration simply on the ground that they are philosophically impure in that they come to us mixed with elements of error. Perhaps the way to truth (a phrase of hope that may be permitted us lightly) cannot thrive on too pure a diet. Perhaps it is not by throwing out all fictive and mythological accretions that truth is best courted. The truest explanation of anything is not necessarily the one that is most efficient or that is most free from incidental error. Perhaps truth, like certain precious metals, is presented best in alloys. In that case the way toward it will be through a guided succession of tentative errors. The metaphoric and the mythic are needed elements in the intellectual life of an individual and of a community; only, when serious questioning begins, one must deal with the proposed answers not by outright acceptance or rejection but with limited and qualified consideration, murmuring with the Hindu gurus of the Upanishads, "*neti neti*"—"not quite that, not quite that!"

Notes

CHAPTER ONE: LANGUAGE AND CONCEPTION

1. The translation in the text follows virtually that of Herman Oulds, whose translation of the *Tao Teh Ching* is published under the title, *The Way of Acceptance* (London: Andrew Dakers, 1946). Other translations of the opening sentence are: "The Tao that can be trodden is not the enduring and unchanging Tao" (James Legge, Vol. XXXIX of *Sacred Books of the East*); "The Tao that can be told of / Is not the Absolute Tao" (Lin Yutang, *The Wisdom of Lao Tse*, The Modern Library, 1958); "The Tao that can be 'tao-ed' can not be the infinite Tao" (Dwight Goddard, *The Buddhist Bible*, 1938; Dutton, 1952); "Existence is beyond the power of words/To define" (Witter Bynner, *The Way of Life according to Laotzu*, Norton, 1944).

2. Friedrich Max Müller, *The Science of Language / founded on lectures delivered at the Royal Institution in 1861 and 1863* (revised edition, Scribner, 1891; 2 vols.). Cf. J. M. Edmonds, *An Introduction*

to Comparative Philology for Classical Students (Cambridge, 1891); Herman H. Bender, *The Home of the Indo-Europeans* (Princeton University Press, 1922).

3. Particularly to be mentioned are the following. On the side of anthropology: Lucien Lévy-Bruhl, *L'expérience mystique et les symboles chez les primitifs* (Paris, 1938). On the side of classical studies: Francis M. Cornford, *From Religion to Philosophy* (Longmans, Green, 1912); Richard B. Onians, *The Origin of European Thought / about the body, the mind, the soul, the world, time, and fate* (Cambridge University Press, 1951; rev. ed., 1954). On the side of philosophy: Ernst Cassirer, *Philosophy of Symbolic Forms* (Yale University Press, 1953-1957): Vol. II, *Mythical Thinking*. In terms of our present vocabulary this volume would be more accurately named *Mythic Thinking*.

CHAPTER TWO: COMMUNICATION

1. My earlier discussion of steno-language can be found in *The Burning Fountain / A Study in the Language of Symbolism* (Indiana University Press, 1954), esp. pp. 25-29, 55-59.

2. St. Augustine, *Confessions*, Bk. I, Chap. viii: "Cum ipsi appellabant rem aliquam et cum secundum eam vocem corpus ad aliquid movebant, videbam et tenebam hoc ab eis vocari rem illam, quod sonabant, cum eam vellent ostendere. . . Ita verba in variis sententiis locis suis posita et crebro audita quarum rerum signa essent paulatim colligebam measque iam voluntates, edomito in eis signis ore, per haec enuntiabam."

3. Plato, *Republic*, Bk. VI, 509D-511B, where he employs the analogy of the Divided Line. The second characteristic of geometrical entities (*"ta mathematika"*) is that "they use images drawn from the world of physical things"—i.e., they come to be intelligible to the mind by means of such images.

4. The view that spatial relations are uniquely susceptible of measurement is now a philosophical commonplace, and is evident from a consideration of exactly how measurement takes place. Cf. Henri Bergson, *Les donnés immédiates de la conscience*: especially pp. 75-99 of the English translation by F. L. Pogson (*Time and Free Will,* Macmillan, 1910).

5. Otto Jesperson, *Mankind, Nation and Individual from a Linguistic Point of View* (Oslo, 1925), p. 97.

6. "Vorausgesetzt, dass die Wahrheit ein Weib ist—wie? ist der Verdacht nicht gegründet, dass alle Philosophen, sofern sie Dogmatiker waren, sich schlecht auf Weiber verstanden?"—Friedrich

Nietzsche, preface to *Jenseits von Gut und Böse* (*Beyond Good and Evil*). Cf. Mallarmé: "Il doît y avoir quelque chose d'occulte au fond de tout." The Lao-tze quotation is the same, but differently translated, as that with which the first chapter begins.

7. The quatrain appeared first in Wallace Stevens, *Parts of a World* (Knopf, 1942); subsequently in *The Collected Poems of Wallace Stevens* (Knopf, 1957). Quoted by permission of the publisher.

CHAPTER THREE: TENSIVE LANGUAGE

1. An amalgam of Fragments 26 and 27, as given in the present author's *Heraclitus* (Princeton University Press, 1959). Subsequent quotations from Heraclitus are drawn from the version there presented. In Bywater's edition, which is followed by a majority of English translators, the fragments here cited are numbered 62 and 63.

2. Mallarmé's declaration was made to Degas, who as an avocation from painting would write sonnets, and who on the occasion in question had spoken to Mallarmé of having "an excellent idea for a poem." The words of Lascelles Abercrombie are taken from his volume, *The Theory of Poetry* (Harcourt, Brace, 1926).

3. Many of Hopkins' best references to the idea of inscape have been assembled in *A Hopkins Reader*, edited by John Pick (Oxford University Press, 1953), esp. pp. 35-67, "Observations of Nature: Inscape." E. g., p. 52: "A bundled heaven, the moon just marked by a blue spot pushing its way through the dark cloud . . . I read a broad careless inscape flowing throughout." In discussing poetry he speaks of "speech which afters and oftens its inscape," p. 83.

4. *The Collected Works of Hart Crane* (Liveright, 1933). Quoted by permission of the publisher.

5. John Masefield, *Poems* (Macmillan, 1953). Quoted by permission of the publisher.

6. T. S. Eliot, *The Complete Poems and Plays, 1909-1950* (Harcourt, Brace, 1952). Quoted by permission of the publisher.

7. Robert Bridges, *The Necessity of Poetry*, Vol. XXVIII of his *Collected Works* (London, Oxford University Press, 1927-1936). William Empson, *Seven Types of Ambiguity* (Chatto and Windus, 1930). Lascelles Abercrombie, *The Theory of Poetry* (Harcourt, Brace, 1926).

8. Elizabeth Drew, *T. S. Eliot/The Design of his Poetry* (Scribner's, 1949), p. 155 and note. Grover Smith, Jr., *T. S. Eliot's Poetry and Plays* (University of Chicago Press, 1956). Brinnin's discussion is in the Appendix to Kimon Friar and John Malcolm Brinnin, *Modern Poetry/American and British* (Appleton-Century-Crofts, 1951).

9. Richard Wilbur, *Things of This World* (Harcourt, Brace, 1956). Quoted by permission of the publisher.

10. Shakespeare, *Antony and Cleopatra*, Act II, Scene ii.

11. C. Day Lewis, *The Poetic Image* (Jonathan Cape, 1947); cf. his *The Poet's Way of Knowledge* (Cambridge University Press, 1957). Ezra Pound, *Make It New* (Yale University Press, 1935), esp. pp. 335-336; cf. his *Gaudier-Brzeska, a Memoir* (London, 1916, 1939); cf. his *ABC of Reading* (Routledge, 1934): the passage on "phanopoeia." Allen Tate, *The Man of Letters in the Modern World* (Meridian Books, 1955), early chapters; cf. *The Forlorn Demon* (Regnery, 1953), chapter on "The Symbolic Imagination."

12. John Middleton Murry, *Countries of the Mind/Essays in Literary Criticism*, Second Series (Oxford University Press, 1931): Chap. I, "Metaphor." Murry describes the world of imagination, not opposed to reality but an extension and deepening of it, as a "world of qualitative interpenetration" (p. 14), and therein as requiring metaphor to express it.

CHAPTER FOUR: TWO WAYS OF METAPHOR

1. *Chuang Tzu, Mystic, Moralist, and Social Reformer*, translated from the Chinese by Herbert A. Giles (Shanghai, 1926), Chap. III.

2. Cf. *The Burning Fountain* (Indiana University Press, 1954), pp. 93-94, 106-112.

3. The sense in which Stevens identifies metaphor with metamorphosis is developed in *The Necessary Angel* (Knopf, 1951), esp. pp. 117-118: "Poetry . . . is almost incredibly the outcome of figures of speech or, what is the same thing, the outcome of the operation of one imagination on another, through the instrumentality of the metaphors. To identify metaphor and metamorphosis is merely to abbreviate [this] remark." The fullest development of the theme of metamorphosis as an essential element of all poetry and as a conscious method in much modern poetry is to be found in Sister M. Bernetta Quinn, O.S.F., *The Metamorphic Tradition in Modern Poetry* (Rutgers University Press, 1955). Cf. Note 8 to Chap. VIII.

4. Aristotle, *Poetics*, Chaps. 21, 22. Cf. his *Rhetoric*, Bk. III, Chaps. 2, 4, 9, 11.

5. Paul Henle, "Metaphor," in *Language, Thought and Culture*, edited by Paul Henle (University of Michigan Press, 1958), Chap. VII.

6. T. E. Hulme, "Autumn"; republished in *Canzoni and Ripostes of Ezra Pound / whereon are appended the complete poetical works of T. E. Hulme* (London, 1913). Richard Wilbur, *Things of This World* (Harcourt, Brace, 1956). The Egyptian verses are found originally together with those on pps. 87-88: see Note 13, this chapter.

7. *The Collected Poems of Dylan Thomas* (New Directions, 1939, 1953). Quoted by permission of the publisher. The Nahuatl poem appears in Irene Richardson, *Fireflies in the Night / A Study of Ancient Mexican Poetry and Symbolism* (Faber and Faber, 1959), p. 18. The Yeats poem can be found in *The Collected Poems of W. B. Yeats* (Macmillan, amplified edition, 1950).

8. "In a Station in the Metro," in Ezra Pound, *Selected Poems*, edited by T. S. Eliot (Faber and Gwyer, 1928), p. 89. The two-line poem should be read in the context established by the quite distinct poems that precede and follow.

9. T. S. Eliot, "The Metaphysical Poets," in *Selected Essays, 1917-1932* (Harcourt, Brace, 1932), p. 247.

10. E[lijah] Jordan, *Essays in Criticism* (University of Chicago Press, 1952), pp. 117, 124, 113. Cf. p. 216: "A metaphor is therefore a constitutional element in a poem, and it is so by virtue of the qualities it creates for its component words through the relationships it sets up among them."

11. Wallace Stevens, "Thirteen Ways of Looking at a Blackbird," originally in *Harmonium* (Knopf, 1923, 1931); subsequently in *The Collected Poems of Wallace Stevens* (Knopf, 1957). Quoted by permission of the publisher.

12. W. H. Auden, "The Fall of Rome," *Nones* (Random House, 1951), pp. 32-33. Quoted by permission of the publisher.

13. Adolf Erman, *The Literature of the Ancient Egyptians*, translated by A. M. Blackman (Methuen, 1927), pp. 1-10. The translation is revised in Josephine Mayer and Tom Prideaux, *Never to Die / the Egyptians in their Own Words* (Viking, 1938), pp. 69-71. The present version is concocted from these two English versions as well as from Erman's German translation from the Egyptian. Quoted by permission of the later publisher.

14. *Tao Teh Ching*, Chap. 11. Cf. Note 1 to Chap. I.

15. *The Poems of Richard Aldington* (Doubleday, Doran, 1928, 1934). Quoted by permission of the publisher.

16. Robert Penn Warren, "Pursuit," in *Selected Poems, 1923-1943* (Harcourt, Brace, 1944). Quoted by permission of the publisher.

CHAPTER FIVE: FROM METAPHOR TO SYMBOL

1. Thomas Carlyle, *Sartor Resartus*: Part III, Chap. III, "Symbolism." Carlyle adds: "And if both the speech be itself high and the silence fit and noble, how expressive will their union be! Thus in many a painted device, or simple seal-emblem, the commonest truth stands out to be proclaimed with quite new emphasis."

The Wallace Stevens remark occurs in his poem, "Man Carrying Thing," in the *Collected Poems*. Perhaps a nuance is lost in the prose setting. The original form is:

> The poem must resist the intelligence
> Almost successfully. . . .

2. William Ralph Inge, *Christian Mysticism* (Methuen, 1899, 1948), p. 5.

3. This and the following Hart Crane quotations are from *The Collected Poems of Hart Crane* (Liveright, 1933). Quoted by permission of the publisher. "Praise for an Urn" and "Garden Abstract" had originally been published in Crane's *White Buildings* (Boni & Liveright, 1926); "Cutty Sark" in *The Bridge* (Liveright, 1930).

4. Northrop Frye, *The Anatomy of Criticism* (Princeton University Press, 1957), p. 100. The quoted remark draws a fuller intelligibility from Professor Frye's connected argument. My admiration for the book is consistent with a refusal to accept the oversimplified distinction between outward and inward directions of meaning, which lead the author to declare (p. 74), "In all literary verbal structures the final direction of meaning is inward." Frye would reject forcibly the vulgar readiness to dismiss all literary evaluations as "merely subjective;" but such readiness draws conceptual support from the quasi-Cartesian dualism of "outward" vs. "inward."

5. The two Elizabethan quotations are respectively from: Lyly's *Campaspe*, Act V, Scene i, in *The Complete Works of John Lyly*, edited by R. Warwick Bond, Vol. II (Oxford: Clarendon Press, 1902); and Kyd's *Cornelia*, Act II, Scene i, in *The Works of Thomas Kyd*, edited by Frederick S. Boas (Oxford: Clarendon Press, 1901).

6. The Old Testament references are to Genesis iii. 8 and iii. 19. The principal New Testament references are to the Gospel of John x. 9 (the Door), vi. 35 (the Bread), xv. 1-5 (the Vine), i. 1, 14 (the Word), and i. 7-9, viii. 12 (the Light).

CHAPTER SIX: THE ARCHETYPAL SYMBOL

1. Arnold van Gennep, *The Rites of Passage* (University of Chicago Press, 1960 [French original, 1909]).

2. Ptah-Hotep, in Mayer and Prideaux, *Never to Die / the Egyptians in their Own Words* (Viking, 1938).

3. G[odfrey] R. Driver, *Semitic Writing from Pictograph to Alphabet* (London, 1948).

4. Heraclitus, Fragment 70 in Bywater (followed by most English

translators), 103 in Diels, and 109 in the present writer's *Heraclitus* (Princeton University Press, 1959), where it is translated, "In the circle the beginning and the end are common." This is literal. But the word ξυνός, besides meaning "common," carries an overtone of ξὺν νῷ "with rational intelligence." On Heraclitus' functional use of the pun, see the Princeton University Press volume, p. 120, note 8, and again p. 148, note to Fragment 81.

5. W. E. Soothill, *The Three Religions of China* (Oxford University Press, 2nd ed., 1923), regards the Lamaist prayer wheel as "a grotesque form of Buddha's lofty conception of the Wheel of the Law rolling forward like the sun and enlightening the world." Charles A. S. Williams, *Outlines of Chinese Symbolism* (Peiping, 1931): "The turning of the wheel of the Law was probably connected with the Vedic sun-worshiping ceremonies in which a chariot wheel was fastened to a post and turned towards the right, i.e. following the path of the Universal Law which directed the sun in its orbit." Cf. E. Dale Saunders, *Mudra* (Bollingen Series XLVIII: Pantheon Books, 1958).

6. Sir Charles Eliot, *Hinduism and Buddhism* (London, 1921), esp. Vol. II, p. 52, and Vol. III, p. 438; Sir Hari Singh Gour, *The Spirit of Buddhism* (London, 1929), p. 166; H. Hackmann, *Buddhism as a Religion* (London, 1910), p. 194; Eugene W. Burlingame, *Buddhist Parables* (Yale University Press, 1922); Charles A. S. Williams, *Encyclopaedia of Chinese Symbols and Art Motives* (New York, Julian Press, 1960), under the entries "Lotus" and "Wheel of the Law." What is briefly called the Lotus Scripture in the text is the *Saddharmapundarika*, traditionally translated "Lotus of the Good Name."

CHAPTER SEVEN: ON THE VERGE OF MYTH

1. Alan W. Watts, *Myth and Ritual in Christianity* (Macmillan, 1954), p. 7.

2. Susanne K. Langer, *Philosophy in a New Key* (Harvard University Press, 1942), esp. Chaps. VI, VII. Ernst Cassirer, *The Philosophy of Symbolic Forms*, Vol. II, "Mythical Thinking" (Yale University Press, 1955).

3. Rudolf Otto, *The Idea of the Holy* (Oxford University Press, 1931), esp. Chaps. II, III.

4. Ovid, *Metamorphoses*, Bk. VIII, 11. 629-724. The charming lightness of the presential mood is well conveyed by Rolfe Humphries' translation (Indiana University Press, 1955). The episode of Aeneas' meeting with Venus, in Bk. I of Vergil's *Aeneid*, is also available in a translation by Humphries (Scribner's, 1951).

5. The characteristic of having created oneself was passed around to various gods in ancient Egypt, but Atum is the one most widely accredited with that unique ability. Khebera, too, is described in the Pyramid Texts as the self-generated one, with the added comment, "Therein dost thou become thy name, 'the Beetle'": see *Ancient Eastern Texts Relating to the Old Testament* (Princeton University Press, 1955), p. 4; cf. James Breasted, *Development of Religion and Thought in Ancient Egypt* (Scribner's, 1912), p. 13. It is stated in the Egyptian *Book of the Dead* that "before the liftings of Shu had taken place"—i.e., before the air-god Shu had pushed the sky up to a place high above the earth—Re stood upon a hill that rose from the primeval waters and created things *by creating their names*. Of himself he declares, "I am the great god . . . who came into being by himself . . . I created my own name."

6. Opposites persistently meet in Tlazolteotl. Julio Jiménez Rueda (*Historia de la Cultura en México*, Mexico City, 1957, pp. 128, 130) calls her a "goddess of uncleanliness" (*diosa de la inmundicia*), who paints her face like a harlot, while her priests do likewise. A French writer, Lucian Biart (*The Aztecs*, Eng. tr. 1900, pp. 135-136) calls her "goddess of trickery" and says of her: "She was the divinity invoked by evil-doers, to obtain not only pardon for their faults but also to escape the infamy that might result therefrom." Biart adds, however, that the penitent had to avoid falling into the same sin a second time, because Tlazolteotl would pardon a sin only once. George Vaillant (*The Aztecs of Mexico*, 1941, p. 180) tends rather to emphasize the moral significance of the goddess, "since in eating refuse she consumed the sins of mankind, leaving them pure. A ritual of confession developed in her cult."

7. Friedrich Max Müller, *The Science of Language* (rev. ed., Scribner's, 1891), Vol. I, p. 21. Müller writes: "Mythology . . . is in truth a disease of language. A myth means a word, but a word which, from being a name or an attribute, has been allowed to assume a more substantial existence." He adds that most names of Greek, Roman, and Hindu gods represent developments of words which "were gradually allowed to assume a divine personality never contemplated by the original inventors."

8. Horatio Hale, " 'Above' and 'Below' / a Mythological Disease of Language," in *Journal of American Folk-Lore*, Vol. III (1890), pp. 177-190. While admitting that Müller's characterization of mythology as a "disease of language" is too sweeping in its generality, Hale affirms that the statement has a partial truth, and in confirmation he examines three American Indian legends, one of which has here been summarized.

9. Sylvanus G. Morley, *The Ancient Maya* (Stanford University Press, 1946), pp. 213-214. In the 1956 edition, revised by Brainerd, this becomes p. 188. Ten pages later Morley adds that Hunab Ku, the creator, "does not appear to have played an important part in the life of the common people, perhaps being regarded by them more as a distant priestly abstraction than as a personal creator."

10. Philological evidence reveals three kinds of concrete experience on which the ancient Indo-European thinker drew when he wanted to express the idea of existence: the experiences of breathing, of dwelling, and of growing. The extreme irregularity of our verb "to be" is thereby largely explained: *asmi*, "I breathe," probably lies back of both "am" and "is"; the root *bhu*, "to grow," lies back of "be"; and the root *vas*, "to dwell," lies back of "was." See F. Max Müller, *Lectures on the Origin and Growth of Religion as Illustrated by the Religion of India* (London, 1878), pp. 191-192.

11. Both of the two passages personifying the relation between sky and earth are quoted by Athenaeus in *The Deipnosophists*, Bk. XIII, Chap. 73. The former passage is from *The Danaids*, a lost play by Aeschylus, and is numbered Fragment 25 in the Loeb Classical Library edition of Aeschylus, Vol. II; it is Fragment 44 in Nauck, *Tragicorum Graecorum Fragmenta*. The latter passage is from an unspecified lost play by Euripides; Aristotle employs it in indirect discourse in Bk. VIII, Chap. i of *The Nicomachean Ethics*.

12. *Rig-Veda*, Bk. VII, Hymns 89, 88, mainly as translated by H. D. Griswold in *The Religion of the Rigveda* (Oxford University Press, 1923), p. 123.

CHAPTER EIGHT: THE SENSE OF REALITY

1. For the Zen Buddhist anecdote I am indebted to Mr. Alan W. Watts. Of his writings on Zen I would recommend particularly *The Spirit of Zen* (London, John Murray, 1936; paper, Grove Press, 1960) and *The Way of Zen* (Pantheon, 1957; paper, Mentor Books, 1959).

2. Mai-Mai Sze, *The Tao of Painting* (Bollingen Series XLIX, Pantheon Books, 1956). These two volumes published in the Bollingen Series, described as "a study of the ritual disposition of Chinese painting," are a delight to the eye and the mind simultaneously; it would be hard to find a more beautiful example of American book making. Volume I is given to an exposition by Mai-Mai Sze of how Chinese painting is related to *Tao* and to *Ch'i* ("heavenly inspiration"), and of "the four treasures"—namely, brush, ink, inkstone, and parchment. Vol. II consists of Miss Sze's translation of the wonderful old Chinese treatise on painting, entitled *The Mustard Seed Garden Manual*.

3. *The Complete Collected Poems of William Carlos Williams, 1906-1938* (New Directions, 1938), p. 127. Quoted by permission of the publisher. The lines constitute Section xxi of *Spring and All* (originally 1923). The personal importance of the red wheelbarrow memory for the poet is shown by his choice of the passage for quotation in his autobiographical reminiscences, *I Wanted to Write a Poem* (Beacon Press, 1958).

4. "Primrose" is from *Sour Grapes*, originally published by The Four Seas Company in 1921; p. 85 of the *Collected Poems*. The four fragments that follow are from *Spring and All* (Chaucer Head); pp. 103-119 of the *Collected Poems*. Quoted by permission of the publisher, New Directions.

5. Edwin Muir, *Collected Poems, 1921-1958* (Faber and Faber, 1959), p. 92. Quoted by permission of the publisher. Stephen Spender's appraisal of "The Wayside Station" appears in his *Poetry since 1939* (Longmans, Green, 1946), p. 27.

6. Cf. Owen Barfield, *Saving the Appearances* (Faber and Faber, 1957), esp. Chaps. I-IV. The appearances that Mr. Barfield seeks to save are the pure qualities of things, their radical suchness, the particular essences that often receive short shrift from those theories that put the main emphasis upon structure and upon standardized methods. What may be called the ontology of the pure *quale* is no new problem, of course; many professional philosophers have wrestled with it. Mr. Barfield, who is not a professional philosopher but an English man of law with an intense awareness of poetry, has long been known for his remarkable study entitled *Poetic Diction* (Faber and Guyer, 1928; Faber and Faber, 1952).

7. The coalescence of the concrete and the abstract in Heraclitus' conception of Fire is discussed in my *Heraclitus* (Princeton University Press, 1959), pp. 14-15, 38-42.

8. Sister M. Bernetta Quinn, *The Metamorphic Tradition in Modern Poetry* (Rutgers University Press, 1955). "Metamorphosis, summarizing as it does man's desire and need to transcend the psychologically repressive conditions of his mechanized milieu, . . . begins and ends the history of man, from baptism to resurrection, affecting the world within him and the world without" (p. 1). Sister Bernetta's mode of analysis enables her to combine the Christian insight of man's finitude confronted by an infinite Reality and the Ovidian metamorphic insight of "forms ever taking new bodies"—that is, of particular essences ever moulding and remoulding themselves into new configurations.

INDEX

Index

IN THE case of words which represent ideas central to the main theme the page numbers will refer only to the most focussed and elucidatory passages. Words followed by "(S)" are employed symbolically.